PUNCTUATE
Like a Pro!

A Student Resource and Writing Workbook

Grades 5-8

By Darlene Dehart Bingham

DEDICATION

To my husband, Greg, and my son, Nick, who encouraged me to pursue my love of teaching and writing. To my friend, Kim, who shared her ideas and helped with editing. To all my students, who inspired me to learn more, so I could teach others how to **PUNCTUATE Like a Pro!**

ACKNOWLEDGEMENT

To all of the wonderful children's authors acknowledged in this book who have written amazing stories that inspire young readers and writers.

Tutortime4kidz Resources

tutortime4kidz@yahoo.com

ISBN-10: 0-9986382-0-X

ISBN-13: 978-0-9986382-0-1

Table of Contents

Table of Contents

Table of Contents

Introduction

Do you ever wonder how your favorite author keeps you glued to the pages of books? Do you want to write amazing sentences and paragraphs like a professional writer? Well, you can!

PUNCTUATE Like a Pro! is a student resource and writing workbook that provides easy to understand punctuation rules, explanations, and examples from well-known children's authors.

What will students learn from this workbook?

Students will learn how to correctly and creatively punctuate words, sentences, and paragraphs. Students will learn to write like a professional author as illustrated in the examples below.

"Welcome!" he said. "Welcome to a new year at Hogwarts! Before we begin our banquet, I would like to say a few words. And here they are: Nitwit! Blubber! Oddment! Tweak! Thank you!"

J. K. Rowling, *Harry Potter and the Sorcerer's Stone*

"Lonely? Ha! Lonely? Not by a long shot. I've got my dog, and when I want to see people I just walk down to the harbor. When I want real quiet, I go on over to Wood Island."

Sharon Creech, *The Wanderer*

He opened the door—and there they were! Beans. Mutto. Henry. Three grinning faces. Shoving wrapped gifts into his chest. Storming past him into his house, Beans bellowing, "Where's the grub?"

Jerry Spinelli, *Wringer*

What does this workbook include?

✓ 15 punctuation marks with easy to understand usage rules.
✓ Clear explanations for using punctuation correctly and creatively.
✓ Examples with bolded text that highlight the punctuation and skill taught.
✓ Learn to write simple, compound, complex, and compound-complex sentences.
✓ Pro Tips (Professional Tips) that teach advanced sentence writing skills.
✓ Over 170 examples from well-known children's authors.
✓ Helpful writing aids and resources to assist students.
✓ Over 70 quick and simple practice assignments.
✓ An answer key to check completed work.
✓ A Punctuation Checklist.

Where Can I Get More Information?

For more information please email us at: tutortime4kidz@yahoo.com

Punctuation Checklist

PUNCTUATION	MARK	HOW TO USE THE PUNCTUATION
Periods	.	• Place at the end of declarative sentences. • Place at the end of some imperative sentences. • Place after some abbreviations.
Exclamation Points	!	• Place at the end of words and sentences to show strong emotion. • Place at the end of strong imperative sentences to show strong feeling. • Place after strong interjections that convey strong feeling or emotion.
Question Marks	?	• Place at the end of words and sentences to indicate a question.
Commas	,	• Use to separate the day of the month from the year. • Use to separate the city name from the state or country name. • Use to separate names of people directly addressed. • Use to separate degrees used with names. • Use to separate coordinate (equal) adjectives. • Use after introductory words, phrases, and dependent clauses. • Use with conjunctive adverbs. • Use after some interjections. • Use to separate words, phrases, and clauses in a series. • Use to separate nonessential words, phrases, and clauses. • Use to separate independent clauses joined by coordinating conjunctions. • Use to separate contrasting words at the end of sentences. • Use to separate interrupting words, phrases, and clauses. • Use to separate dialogue from the dialogue tag.
Semicolons	;	• Use to join independent clauses when a coordinating conjunction and comma is **not** used. • Use to join independent clauses when a conjunctive adverb is used. • Use to replace commas in sentences with lists to eliminate confusion.
Colons	:	• Use after a main clause or sentence that introduces a list. • Use after a main clause or sentence that introduces more information. • Use after a main clause or sentence that introduces a formal quote. • Use to separate hours and minutes in clock time. • Use after greetings in business letters.
Quotation Marks	" "	• Use around dialogue and words quoted. • Use around slang words and expressions. • Use around titles of shorter works of writing (poems, songs, articles).
Single Quotation Marks	' '	• Use to indicate a quote within a quote.
Italicizing	*good*	• Use for titles of longer works of writing (books, magazines, newspapers). • Use for specific names given to vehicles, paintings, and sculptures. • Use to indicate the internal thoughts of characters. • Use to emphasize words and phrases.
Parentheses	( )	• Use around words or phrases to add information, explain, or clarify. • Use around numbers or letters when listing information.
Brackets	[ ]	• Use to insert letters or words in quoted material.
Ellipses	...	• Use to indicate a drop off of speech or trailing off of thought. • Use to indicate that words have been eliminated from a quote.
Dashes	—	• Use to emphasize a word or words. • Use to show an interruption in speech or sudden change of thought.
Hyphens	-	• Use when spelling fractions and numbers twenty-one to ninety-nine. • Use to separate spans of numbers and words spelled out. • Use to separate some compound words and prefixes from root words. • Use to separate syllables and letters joined to words.
Apostrophes	'	• Use to show possession (ownership). • Use in contractions to indicate letters have been removed.

5

Periods End Declarative Sentences

Use periods at the end of declarative sentences. A declarative sentence makes a statement.

Pa was whistling while he climbed to the wagon-seat and took up the reins.
Laura Ingalls Wilder, *Little House on the Prairie*

Brian felt his eyes beginning to burn and knew there would be tears.
Gary Paulsen, *Hatchet*

Mother sat down at the table and put her head in her hands.
James Lincoln Collier and Christopher Collier, *My Brother Sam is Dead*

Punctuate It
Place a period at the end of each declarative sentence below.

1. The Pacific Ocean is the largest ocean on Earth

2. The two longest rivers in the world are the Nile and the Amazon

3. Mount Everest is the tallest mountain in the world

4. George Washington was the first president of the United States

Write It
Write 2 declarative sentences ending with a period.

1. _____

_____

2. _____

_____

Periods End Some Imperative Sentences

Use periods at the end of some imperative sentences. An imperative sentence gives a command or a strong request. The sentence often begins with a verb and has no subject because the subject is understood. Imperative sentences may also end with an exclamation point (see Exclamation Points page 11).

"Steady pace, now," he said. "Don't look frightened, whatever you do."
C. S. Lewis, *The Silver Chair*

"Never stand next to someone with a *G* in her number."
Jane Yolen, *The Devil's Arithmetic*

"Wait a minute," Spangler said. "Sit down. Take it easy."
William Saroyan, *The Human Comedy*

Punctuate It
Place a period at the end of each imperative sentence below.

1. Stop the bus at the next corner

2. Eat all of your meat and vegetables

3. Turn out the lights and close the door when you leave

4. Please go straight home after school

Write It
Write 2 imperative sentences ending with a period.

1. _____

_____

2. _____

_____

Periods After Abbreviations

Use periods after some abbreviations. Abbreviations are shortened forms of words. Do not abbreviate state names, days of the week, or months used in sentences.

Example: Dr. Scott's office opens on Monday, August 30, at 8:00 a.m.

Abbreviation Type	Examples of Abbreviations
Titles Before Names	Capt. (Captain)　Dr. (Doctor)　Gen. (General)　Mr. (Mister)　Mrs. (Mistress)　Prof. (Professor)　Rev. (Reverend)　St. (Saint)
Titles After Names	D.D.S. (Doctor of Dental Surgery)　Jr. (Junior)　Sr. (Senior)　M.D. (Medical Doctor)　Ph.D. (Doctor of Philosophy)
Initials in Names	J. L. Smith (Jay Lee Smith)　R. Chin (Raymond Chin)
Days of the Week	Mon.　Tues.　Wed.　Thurs.　Fri.　Sat.　Sun.
Months of the Year	Jan. Feb. Mar. Apr. May June July Aug. Sept. Oct. Nov. Dec.
Addresses	Ave. (Avenue)　Blvd. (Boulevard)　Ct. (Court)　Dr. (Drive)　Rd. (Road)　St. (Street)　P.O. Box (Post Office Box)
Companies	Co. (Company)　Inc. (Incorporated)　Org. (Organization)
Time	A.M. or a.m. (ante meridiem-before noon)　P.M. or p.m. (post meridiem-after noon)　yr. (year)　sec. (second)　min. (minute)　hr. (hour)　B.C. (before Christ)　A.D. (Anno Domini)　C.E. (Common Era)　B.C.E. (Before Common Era)

It's now one **A.M.**, a wave has just filled the cockpit, and I'm on watch. Please let the wind die down.

Sharon Creech, *The Wanderer*

Mrs. Rachel was one of those delightful and popular people who pride themselves on speaking their mind without fear of favor.

Lucy Maud Montgomery, *Anne of Green Gables*

Joe had a cousin with a **Ph.D.** in corvidology, and she was as wacky as he was.

Lilian Jackson Braun, *The Cat Who Had 60 Whiskers*

Punctuate It

Write the correct abbreviation for each word below.

1. Mister_____　　　**3.** Doctor_____　　　**5.** Saint_____

2. Senior_____　　　**4.** Avenue_____　　　**6.** October_____

Pro Tip: Use Periods After a Word or Words

Some fiction writers use periods at the end of a word of words. This would be similar to using an interjection (see Interjections page 12). The words are not complete sentences, and they would normally not stand alone. Notice in the examples below how the professional authors place periods after a word or words to emphasize the word or get to a point quickly.

If they'd gone, he knew where she'd be. Sitting at the kitchen table. Alone in the dark. **Crying.**

Susan Collins, *Gregor the Overlander*

Then he leaned toward me and said with a warm smile, *"Bienvenida. **Welcome.**"*

Jennifer Cervantes, *Tortilla Sun*

He opened the door—and there they were! **Beans. Mutto. Henry.** Three grinning faces. Shoving wrapped gifts into his chest.

Jerry Spinelli, *Wringer*

Punctuate It

Place periods after the word or words in the sentences below. Each sentence requires 2 or more commas.

1. One by one the students fell asleep First Jeff Then Sal and Kira.

2. Trina ate the noodles but left the green things Peas Broccoli Yuk!

3. The lights began to flicker On Off On Off.

4. Breathe in Breathe out Deep breath Good job!

Write It

Write 2 sentences with a word or words that end with a period. Use this technique to emphasize or get to the point quickly.

1. _____

_____

2. _____

_____

Exclamation Points End Exclamatory Sentences

Use exclamation points at the end of exclamatory sentences. An exclamatory sentence expresses surprise, strong feeling, or excitement.

"It's slowing down, Spiker, it's slowing down! But it hasn't stopped yet! You watch it!"

Roald Dahl, *James and the Giant Peach*

"What a horse, Henry! We've been going around that field like the wind!"
Walter Farley, *The Black Stallion*

"These Amoses had hot water running right into the house!"
Christopher Paul Curtis, *Bud, Not Buddy*

Punctuate It
Place an exclamation point at the end of each exclamatory sentence below.

1. The barking dog chased Ben all the way home

2. Thomas misplaced his wallet and his car keys

3. Nick and Erin won a million dollars in the lottery last night

4. Sue couldn't believe she had won the spelling bee

Write It
Write 2 exclamatory sentences that express surprise, strong feeling, or excitement. Place an exclamation point at the end of each sentence.

1. _____

_____

2. _____

_____

Exclamation Points End Strong Imperative Sentences

Use exclamation points at the end of strong imperative sentences. An imperative sentence gives a command or a strong request. The sentence usually begins with a verb and has no subject. Imperative sentences can also end with periods (see Periods page 7).

"Stop!" Aunt Spiker said quickly. "Hold everything!"

Roald Dahl, *James and the Giant Peach*

"Be quiet!" I shouted, putting my hand over his jaws.

Scott O'Dell, *Island of the Blue Dolphin*

"Stand up!" He was yelling even more loudly.

Elie Wiesel, *Night*

Punctuate It

Place an exclamation point at the end of each imperative sentence below.

1. Pack your bags and get out this minute

2. Catch the baseball

3. Watch out for that car

4. Hurry up and get ready for school

Write It

Write 2 imperative sentences that convey strong feeling or emotion. Place an exclamation point at the end of each sentence.

1. _____

_____

2. _____

_____

Exclamation Points After Strong Interjections

Use exclamation points after strong interjections. Interjections are words that convey strong feeling or emotion. Interjections may also be followed by a comma (see Commas page 25).

Examples of Interjections: ah, awesome, bravo, cheers, congratulations, cool, fabulous, fantastic, good, great, ha, hello, hey, hi, huh, no, no way, oh, oh no, okay, right, sure, thanks, uh-huh, well, whew, wow, yahoo, yeah, yes, yippee

"**Well!**" exclaimed the Wart. "What a cheat! I wouldn't have thought it of him."
T. H. White, *The Sword in the Stone*

"**Oh!**" said Boots, scurrying to her roaches. "**Oh!**"
Suzanne Collins, *Gregor the Overlander*

"**Whew!** And the race is Saturday," said Henry.
Walter Farley, *The Black Stallion*

Punctuate It

Place an exclamation point after the interjection in each sentence below.

1. Awesome Our science project won first place.

2. Bravo Bravo That was a wonderful speech.

3. Oh no I tripped and dropped my computer.

4. Yes Yes We won the dance competition.

Write It

Write 2 sentences with interjections expressing strong feeling or emotion. Place an exclamation point after each interjection.

1. _____

_____

2. _____

_____

Pro Tip: Use Exclamation Points with Repetition

Use exclamation points after repetitive words and phrases. Notice in the passages below how the professional authors use repetition to emphasize a point, provide humor, or create a dramatic effect.

"Move it, move it, move it!" instructed Ripred, herding them all from the open bank and into a tunnel.

Suzanne Collins, *Gregor the Overlander*

"Nicely done, nicely done!" cried the goose. "Try it again, try it again!"

E.B. White, *Charlotte's Web*

"Rum," he repeated. "I must get away from here. Rum! Rum!"

Robert Louis Stevenson, *Treasure Island*

"Won't, won't, won't, WON'T!"

J.K. Rowling, *Harry Potter and the Half-Blood Prince*

Punctuate It

Place exclamation points after the repetition in each sentence below. Each sentence requires more than one exclamation point.

1. Go get help Go Go Go

2. Never Never Never in a hundred years

3. We discovered gold Gold Precious gold

4. We're rich We're rich Rich Rich Rich

Write It

Write 2 sentences using repetition to emphasize a point, provide humor, or create a dramatic effect. Place an exclamation point after the repetition.

1. _____

_____

2. _____

_____

Question Marks End Interrogative Sentences

> **Use question marks after words or interrogative sentences that ask a question.**

"Why? What? Why not?" asked Gregor, feeling his insides go icy.
Suzanne Collins, Gregor the Overlander

"What part of the art room were they standing in?" Sandy said.
Muriel Spark, *The Prime of Miss Jean Brodie*

"Why not use something that rhymes?" suggested Sue.
Beverly Cleary, *Jean and Johnny*

Punctuate It

Place a question mark at the end of each interrogative sentence below.

1. What time does the basketball game start tonight

2. Can Ricardo pick up bananas at the grocery store

3. Do you know how to bake chocolate chip cookies

4. Why Why can't I go to the football game

Write It

Write 2 interrogative sentences. Place a question mark at the end of each sentence.

1. _____

_____

2. _____

_____

Pro Tip: Use Questions to Hook the Reader

Use questions to "hook" the reader. Questions can be used throughout your writing to keep the reader's interest. Notice in the passages below how the professional authors use interesting questions that "hook" or grab the reader's attention.

What would happen when the rest of Gryffindor found out what they'd done?
J. K. Rowling, *Harry Potter and the Sorcerer's Stone*

"Have you ever seen a giant?" asked Merlyn softly, so as not to interrupt the reading.
T. H. White, *The Sword in the Stone*

"What are you saying? Get ready for the journey? What journey? Why? What is happening? Have you gone mad?"
Elie Wiesel, *Night*

D for what, Alex wondered. Danger? Discovery? Or disaster? Only time would tell.
Anthony Horowitz, *Stormbreaker*

That made Father shout. "Free? Free to do what, Sam? Free to mock your King? To shoot your neighbor? To make a mess of thousands of lives? Where have you been getting these ideas?"
James Lincoln Collier and Christopher Collier, *My Brother Sam is Dead*

Write It

Write 2 interrogative sentences that "hook" or grab the reader's attention. Place a question mark at the end of each sentence.

1. _____

_____

_____

2. _____

_____

_____

Review: Periods, Exclamation Points, and Question Marks

Use periods, question marks, or exclamation points after words and at the end of sentences.

Punctuate It

Read each sentence below and add the correct punctuation. Some of the sentences require more than one punctuation mark.

1. Wow That was the best movie I have ever seen
2. Do you know what time the bus arrives
3. Watch out The huge bear is running our way
4. Alec and Megan will go snow skiing today
5. Will Jane and Chuck attend the volleyball clinic
6. Yahoo Janelle made it to the top of the hill
7. Mrs Martell asked everyone to turn in their homework
8. Where should we go for lunch
9. Please Please Please let me go to the game
10. Carol and Michael attended the jazz concert
11. What time should we leave for our appointment
12. Nick and Erin walked Ollie for one mile
13. Ouch I twisted my ankle
14. No No No I won't do it

Write It

Use what you have learned to write a paragraph (4-5 sentences) using different types of sentences and punctuation. Use short, medium, and long sentences.

_____

_____

_____

_____

_____

_____

Commas Separate Days and Years

Use commas to separate the day of the month from the year. When the date is in the beginning or middle of the sentence, place a comma after the day of the month and after the year.

It was just after dawn on **December 7, 1941,** when 353 Japanese planes came screaming out of the sky over the U.S. naval base at Pearl Harbor.

Tod Olson, *Lost in the Pacific, 1942*

I climbed into my bunk, above my father, who was still alive. The date was **January 28, 1945**.

Elie Wiesel, *Night*

And according to the waitress, it was 9 A.M. on **December 21,** the winter solstice, which gave them three hours until Enceladus's deadline.

Rick Riordan, *The Heroes of Olympus, The Lost Hero*

Note: When the day of the month is missing, do **not** use a comma. **Example:** Joey will graduate in May 2020.

Punctuate It

Add commas to separate the day of the month and the year in each sentence below. Some sentences require two commas.

1. Abraham Lincoln was born on February 12 1809 in Kentucky.

2. Lincoln was elected president on November 6 1860.

3. On January 1 1863 President Lincoln issued the Emancipation Proclamation.

4. The Declaration of Independence was signed on July 4 1776.

Write It

Write 2 sentences using commas to separate the day of the month and the year from the rest of the sentence.

1. _____

_____

2. _____

_____

Commas Separate Cities from States or Countries

Use commas to separate the city name from the state or country name. When the city, state, or country name is in the beginning or middle of the sentence, place a comma after the city name and after the state or country name.

His parents had been dirt-poor when they arrived in **Columbus, Ohio,** from Switzerland.

Todd Olson, *Lost in the Pacific, 1942*

He had done learned carpentry back up there near **Macon, Georgia,** where he was born.

Mildred D. Taylor, *Roll of Thunder, Hear My Cry*

The book listed hundreds of attractions you could visit, from the world's largest ball of twine in **Darwin, Minnesota,** to the world's largest ball of stamps in **Omaha, Nebraska.**

John Green, *Paper Towns*

Punctuate It

Add commas in each sentence below to separate the city name from the state or country name. Some sentences require two commas.

1. The White House is located in Washington D.C.

2. President Obama was born in Honolulu Hawaii in 1961.

3. Disneyland Park is located in Anaheim California.

4. Paris France is the most popular tourist city in the world.

Write It

Write 2 sentences using commas to separate the city name from the state or country name. When the city, state, or country name is in the beginning or middle of the sentence, place a comma after the city name and after the state or country name.

1. _____

_____

2. _____

_____

Commas Separate Names of People Directly Addressed

Use commas in dialogue to separate the names of people directly addressed (directly spoken to) from the rest of the sentence. When the name of the person addressed appears in the middle of the sentence, place commas before and after the name.

"Can't be helped, **Marmee,** so you must resign yourself to all sorts of worries, and let your birds hop out of the nest, one by one."
Louisa May Alcott, *Little Women*

"I could scarcely have missed an opportunity to break bread with you, **Ripred,**" said Solovet.
Suzanne Collins, *Gregor the Overlander*

"**Marilla Cuthbert,** you don't say so!" said Mrs. Spencer in distress.
Lucy Maud Montgomery, *Anne of Green Gables*

Punctuate It
Place commas separating the name of the person directly addressed from the rest of the clause in each sentence below.

1. "Can you pick me up at noon Lucy?" asked Gin.

2. "If you want Jon I can help you," offered Maria.

3. "Sam will you mow the lawn today?"

4. "Are you home yet Jana?" asked Annie.

Write It
Write 2 sentences using commas to separate the name of the person directly addressed from the rest of the sentence.

1. _____

_____

2. _____

_____

Commas Separate Degrees Used with Names

Use commas to separate the name of the person from their degree. Place a comma after the name and after the degree when they appear in the beginning or middle of the sentence. When the name and degree are at the end of the sentence, place a comma between the name and the degree.

Examples of Degrees: D.D.S. (Doctor of Dental Surgery), M.B.A. (Master of Business Administration), M.D. (Medical Doctor), Ph.D. (Doctor of Philosophy), R.N. (Registered Nurse)

Jon Ling, **D.D.S.,** is a respected dental surgeon in our town.

My favorite college professor was Katherine Doyle, **Ph.D.**

Mariel Sanchez, **R.N.,** worked at the local health clinic.

Punctuate It

Place commas to separate the name from the degree in each sentence below. Some sentences require two commas.

1. Julio Martinez D.D.S. is the best dental surgeon in our town.

2. Rina Singh R.N. received her nursing degree in 2014.

3. Susan Crow Ph.D. gave an amazing lecture last week.

4. Our family doctor is Jamal James M.D.

Write It

Write 2 sentences using commas to separate the name of the person from their degree. When the name and degree appear in the beginning or middle of the sentence, place commas before and after the degree.

1. _____

_____

2. _____

_____

Commas After Introductory Words

Use commas after introductory words in a sentence. Introductory words introduce the reader to the main clause or sentence that follows.

Examples of Introductory Words: after, after a while, after that, an hour later, at last, during the summer, earlier that day, finally, first, half an hour later, last, later, later that day, next, secondly, soon, the next day, the next morning, then

"**First,** because I'm on the same side of the door as you are: **secondly,** because they're making such a noise inside, no one could possibly hear you."
Lewis Carroll, *Alice's Adventures in Wonderland*

An hour later, I got tired of waiting for Mateo to show up, so I went looking for him.
Jennifer Cervantes, *Tortilla Sun*

Then, at last, with his stomach turning on the berries, Brian went to sleep.
Gary Paulsen, *Hatchet*

Punctuate It
Place a comma after the introductory words in each sentence below.

1. Finally Corey worked his way to the front of the lunch line.

2. Before long Jamison reached the top of the huge hill.

3. After a long wait Ming decided to walk home.

4. First we have to mix the cake batter with the eggs.

Write It
Write 2 sentences using an introductory word or words. Place a comma after the introductory word or words.

1. _____

_____

2. _____

_____

Commas After Introductory Adjectives

Use commas after introductory adjectives that modify (describe) the main clause or sentence that follows. Adjectives are words that modify or describe nouns and pronouns. Adjectives often tell what kind, what color, how many, or which one.

Examples of Adjectives Describing What Kind: huge, round, small, soft, tall, tiny

Examples of Adjectives Describing Colors: blue, pink, red, turquoise, yellow

Examples of Adjectives Describing How Many: one, five, six, ten, thirty, twenty

Examples of Adjectives Describing Which One: each, that, this, those

Exhausted, hungry, and thirsty, we were led into our stable by Emilie's grandfather, who said not a word but saw to us quickly before hurrying back across the yard to the house.

Michael Morpurgo, *War Horse*

Tall, blond, aged about fifty, Sir Francis Cromarty had played a highly distinguished role during the last Indian Mutiny.

Jules Verne, *Around the World in Eighty Days*

Friendless, dejected, and hungry, he threw himself down in the manure and sobbed.

E. B. White, *Charlotte's Web*

Punctuate It

Place a comma after the introductory adjectives in each sentence below. Some sentences require three commas.

1. Exhausted cold and wet the hiker shuffled through the deep snow.

2. Tired and muddy Mateo wiped the sweat from his brow.

3. Tiny fragile and afraid Mina froze as the shadowy figure approached.

4. Stronger now Edison felt he could conquer the world.

Write It

Write 2 sentences with an introductory adjective or adjectives followed by a comma.

1. _____

_____

2. _____

_____

Commas After Introductory Adverbs

Use commas after introductory adverbs that modify (describe) the main clause or sentence that follows. Adverbs are words that modify verbs, adjectives, and other adverbs. Adverbs often tell **how, when, where, how much,** or **how often.**

Examples of Adverbs Describing How: carefully, loudly, nicely, quietly, slowly

Examples of Adverbs Describing When: early, later, soon, tomorrow, yesterday

Examples of Adverbs Describing Where: here, inside, outside, somewhere

Examples of Adverbs Describing How Much: completely, fully, partially, very

Examples of Adverbs Describing How Often: always, frequently, never, sometimes

Slowly, sadly, poor James got up off the ground and went back to the woodpile.
Roald Dahl, *James and the Giant Peach*

Inside, the walls were whitewashed and the floor unpainted.
John Steinbeck, *Of Mice and Men*

Quickly, they flung a rope with a hook towards him.
J. R. R. Tolkien, *The Hobbit*

Punctuate It
Place a comma after the introductory adverbs in each sentence below.

1. Cautiously the hikers climbed up the steep mountain.

2. Quietly Jonah read the last few chapters of the book.

3. Happily Sheila helped her mother wash the dinner dishes.

4. Slowly and tiredly David walked off the soccer field.

Write It
Write 2 sentences with an introductory adverb or adverbs followed by a comma.

1. _____

_____

2. _____

_____

Commas Used with Conjunctive Adverbs

Use commas with conjunctive adverbs. Conjunctive adverbs can be used like conjunctions to transition between words and sentences. They can also be used to join independent clauses (see Semicolons page 50). When the conjunctive adverb is in the beginning of the sentence, place a comma after the adverb. When the conjunctive adverb is in the middle of the sentence like an interrupter, place commas before and after the adverb.

Examples of Conjunctive Adverbs: additionally, almost, also, anyway, as a result, besides, certainly, consequently, conversely, currently, equally, eventually, finally, furthermore, however, in addition, in fact, indeed, instead, likewise, meanwhile, nevertheless, otherwise, similarly, still, subsequently, that is, then, therefore

However, I did notice that he was moving rather wearily and sluggishly, that each step as we went up was becoming more and more of an effort for him.

Michael Morpurgo, *War Horse*

Therefore, since I have outread him, I see no reason why I cannot outwit and outbox him.

Sid Fleischman, *By the Great Horn Spoon!*

Hester Prynne, **meanwhile,** kept her place upon the pedestal of shame, with glazed eyes, and an air of early indifference.

Nathaniel Hawthorne, *The Scarlet Letter*

Punctuate It

Place commas separating the conjunctive adverb from the main clause in each sentence below. Some sentences require more than one comma.

1. The basketball team in fact was ranked number one.

2. Therefore everyone came to watch the game.

3. Consequently there weren't enough seats for all of the fans.

4. Additional seating finally was added in the gymnasium.

Write It

Write 2 sentences with conjunctive adverbs. Use commas to separate the conjunctive adverb from the main sentence.

1. _____

_____

2. _____

_____

Commas Used with Interjections

Use commas to separate interjections from the rest of the sentence. Interjections are words that convey strong feeling or emotion. When the interjection is part of the sentence, use a comma to separate it from the main clause or sentence. Strong interjections may also be followed by an exclamation point (see Exclamation Points page 12).

Examples of Interjections: ah, awesome, bravo, cheers, cool, fabulous, fantastic, good job, great, ha, hello, hey, hi, hurray, no, no way, oh, oh no, oh well, okay, right, sure, thanks, way to go, well, whew, wow, yahoo, yeah, yes, yippee

"**Ah,** that depends on who wears the apron!" and Laurie gave an audacious tweak at the tassel.

Louisa May Alcott, *Little Women*

"**Oh,** Merlyn," exclaimed the Wart without answering, "please give me something to do, because I feel so miserable."

T. H. White, *The Sword in the Stone*

"**Well,** they were a lazy lot—that much you can't deny."

Mary Norton, *The Borrowers*

Punctuate It
Place a comma after the interjection in each sentence below.

1. Hey let's go to the movies today.

2. Oh no I can't go swimming because I have soccer practice.

3. Well we can all go on vacation together in July.

4. Huh what did you say?

Write It
Write 2 sentences using commas to separate introductory interjections from the main clause or sentence.

1. _____

_____

2. _____

_____

Commas After Introductory Participles and Participial Phrases

Use commas after introductory participles or participial phrases that modify (describe) the main clause or sentence that follows. Participles are formed by adding *–ing, –ed, –en,* or *–n* to the end of a verb. The participle functions as an adjective to modify a noun or pronoun in the sentence that follows.

Examples of Participles: *blowing* wind, *broken* arm, *buried* treasure, *crying* baby, *drifting* snow, *injured* hiker, *painted* wagon, *running* water *winning* team

Examples of Participial Phrases: *Buried* deep beneath the earth, *Crying* at the top of his lungs, *Feeling* happy and satisfied, *Hoping* to find the gold, *Running* as fast as she could, *Startled* by the loud gunshot, *Terrified* of the barking dog

Terrified, I knew I could not run, for there was nowhere to go, so I put my back to him, and lashed out behind me.

Michael Morpurgo, *War Horse*

Seeing the sun shining down and the black shadows drifting over the walls, Rontu barked, then began to howl.

Scott O'Dell, *Island of the Blue Dolphin*

Dazed, suffering intolerable pain from throat and tongue, with the life half throttled out of him, Buck attempted to face his tormenters.

Jack London, *The Call of the Wild*

Punctuate It
Place a comma after each introductory participial phrase below.

1. Facing his fears Jerome climbed back on the wild bronco.

2. Realizing he was lost Hiram sat down and waited for help.

3. Seated quietly at her desk Nan tried to solve the math problem.

4. Running to the sink Austin washed the mud off of his dirty hands.

Write It
Write 2 sentences beginning with introductory participial phrases. Place a comma after each participial phrase.

1. _____

_____

2. _____

_____

Commas After Introductory Prepositional Phrases

Use commas after long (usually 4 or more words) introductory prepositional phrases. A prepositional phrase is a group of words that begins with a preposition and ends with a noun or pronoun.

Examples of Prepositions: about, above, across, after, along, around, as, at, before, behind, below, beneath, beside, between, beyond, by, down, during, except, for, from, in, inside, into, like, near, of, off, on, onto, outside, over, past, through, to, toward, under, up, with, within

Examples of Prepositional Phrases: *after* a long time, *before* nightfall, *beyond* the horizon, *down* by the river, *toward* the end of the day, *with* nowhere to run

During the first few days after the gentleman's departure, considerable sums had been wagered on the chances of his enterprise.

Jules Verne, *Around the World in Eighty Days*

With a sudden flick, quick as lightning, an apple left his hand and hit Bill square on the nose.

J. R. R. Tolkien, *The Lord of the Rings*

After their adventure at the public library, Lionel and Ulysses continued to explore Ithaca.

William Saroyan, *The Human Comedy*

Punctuate It

Place a comma after the introductory prepositional phrase in each sentence below.

1. With perfect form Saraya completed her swan dive.

2. In the final analysis we agreed that her dive was the best.

3. At the end of the day the judges awarded her first prize.

4. With a wide grin she proudly displayed her trophy.

Write It

Write 2 sentences with long introductory prepositional phrases. Place a comma after each phrase.

1. _____

_____

2. _____

_____

Commas After Introductory Dependent Clauses

Use commas after introductory dependent clauses. A dependent clause is a group of words with a subject and a predicate (verb), but the clause cannot stand alone. Introductory dependent clauses usually begin with a subordinating conjunction.

Examples of Subordinating Conjunctions: after, although, as, as soon as, because, before, even, even though, if, now that, once, since, so that, than, though, unless, until, when, whenever, where, wherever, whether, while

As the dismayed driver opened the rear emergency exit, the rain poured down upon him in sharp-needled darts.

Mildred D. Taylor, *Roll of Thunder, Hear My Cry*

Whenever the sound of the wind died away, Laura could faintly hear the noise of that wild jamboree in the Indian camp.

Laura Ingalls Wilder, *Little House on the Prairie*

When we came back from our voyage to Tall Rock, I hid the canoe in the cave below the headland.

Scott O'Dell, *Island of the Blue Dolphin*

Punctuate It

Place a comma after the introductory dependent clause in each sentence below.

1. After Owen completed his assignment he went to lunch.

2. Because it was raining Violet brought her umbrella to school.

3. While Sonya cleaned the table her sister washed the dishes.

4. Since Rylan's team won the game they celebrated at the pizza parlor.

Write It

Write 2 sentences beginning with dependent clauses. Place a comma after each dependent clause.

1. _____

_____

2. _____

_____

Commas Between Coordinate (Equal) Adjectives

Use commas between coordinate (equal) adjectives. Coordinate adjectives equally modify or describe the same noun. To determine if the adjectives are coordinate, try reversing them. If the sentence flows well and makes sense, then the adjectives are most likely coordinate and should be separated with a comma.

Examples: The opera singer sang in a **soft, low** voice.

The opera singer sang in a **low, soft** voice. *Adjectives reversed.*

Later, when the fog rolled along in **deeper, darker** clumps, I imagined great big tiger feet loping toward us—**soft, furry, graceful** tiger feet.

Sharon Creech, *The Wanderer*

To Palmer, **tall, gangly** Henry did not look like a bird at all, but a giraffe with two howling hyenas snapping at its knees.

Jerry Spinelli, *Wringer*

A **small, warm** breeze blew across the compound.

Jane Yolen, *The Devil's Arithmetic*

Punctuate It

Place a comma separating the coordinate adjectives in each sentence below. Each sentence requires one comma.

1. The warm sweet sugar cookie tasted delicious.

2. Mindy hugged the sweet tiny kitten.

3. Sophia shaped the soft cool clay into round balls.

4. The loud playful monkey swung from limb to limb.

Write It

Write 2 sentences using commas to separate coordinate (equal) adjectives.

1. _____

_____

2. _____

_____

Pro Tip: Placement of Multiple Modifiers

Use multiple modifiers (adjectives and adverbs) to increase descriptive information. Modifiers should be placed close to the word or words they describe. Notice how the professional authors place multiple modifiers in the beginning, middle, and end of sentences to help emphasize words, increase descriptive information, and make the sentence more interesting.

The head was that of the wildest of all wild creatures—a stallion born wild—and it was **beautiful, savage, splendid.**

Walter Farley, *The Black Stallion*

Friendless, dejected, and hungry, he threw himself down in the manure and sobbed.

E. B. White, *Charlotte's Web*

Slowly, carefully, she built up the nest until she was sitting on a big grassy mound.

E. B. White, *The Trumpet of the Swan*

They tramped off, **anxious and downhearted,** under the eyes of the crowd.

J. R. R Tolkien, *The Lord of the Rings*

Punctuate It

Place any -ly adverb or an appropriate adjective in each sentence below.

1. _____ , _____ , the rescuers scaled the steep cliff.

    (Adverb)   (Adverb)

2. _____ , _____ , Avery finished the gardening.

    (Adverb)   (Adverb)

3. Tristan watched the _____ , _____ man enter the room.

                  (Adjective)   (Adjective)

4. The children drank the fruit juice, _____ and _____ .

                            (Adjective)   (Adjective)

Write It

Write 2 sentences placing multiple modifiers in the beginning, middle, or end of the sentences. Place commas as needed to separate the modifiers.

1. _____

_____

2. _____

_____

Commas Separate Words in a Series

Use commas to separate words in a series. A series is a list of three or more words separated by commas. Place a comma after each word listed. Place a coordinating conjunction (and, or, but) after the last comma.

Bleeding, bruised, and **terrified** beyond belief, I longed only to be with Topthorn again.
Michael Morpurgo, *War Horse*

Sailors of different **nationalities, shopkeepers, brokers, porters,** and **fellahs** were arriving in large numbers.
Jules Verne, *Around the World in Eighty Days*

He ordered the best hay with **plenty of oats, crushed beans, and bran**, with vetches, or rye grass, as the man might think needful.
Anna Sewell, *Black Beauty*

Punctuate It

Place commas separating the words in a series in each sentence below.

1. Serena Sasha and Tina play on the same softball team.

2. Mom bought vanilla chocolate and strawberry ice cream.

3. Benjamin Franklin was an author printer scientist and politician.

4. Greg taught the puppy to sit stay and heel.

Write It

Write 2 sentences using commas to separate words in a series. Place a comma after each word listed. Place a coordinating conjunction (and, or, but) after the last comma.

1. _____

_____

2. _____

_____

Commas Separate Phrases in a Series

> Use commas to separate three or more phrases in a series. A phrase is a group of related words with no subject or predicate (verb). Place a comma after each phrase listed. Use a coordinating conjunction (and, or, but) after the last comma.

A moment was allowed for the first thrill to subside, **then Hugo, the villain, stalked in with a clanking sword at his side, a slouched hat, black beard, mysterious cloak, and the boots**.

Louisa May Alcott, Little Women

The memory of **the hot breath, the pawing hooves, the rank odor, and the dreadful hiss** was terrifying to her.

Lois Lowry, Gosamer

He was soon in the midst of a crowd of boys who were **running, jumping, playing at ball and leap-frog, and otherwise disporting themselves, and right noisily**, too.

Mark Twain, The Prince and the Pauper

Punctuate It

Place commas to separate the phrases in a series in each sentence below.

1. Pablo grabbed his lunch lined up and walked to the cafeteria.

2. Tam raised her hand answered the question and patted herself on the back.

3. Stefan jumped on his bike rode down the street and turned left at the corner.

4. Haley dug a hole planted seeds and covered the seeds with soil.

Write It

Write 2 sentences using commas to separate phrases in a series. Place a comma after each phrase listed. Use a coordinating conjunction (and, or, but) after the last comma.

1. _____

_____

2. _____

_____

Commas Separate Independent Clauses in a Series

Use **commas** to separate three or more independent clauses (sentences) in a series. Place a comma followed by a coordinating conjunction after each clause listed. A semicolon followed by a conjunctive adverb or a single semicolon can also be used to join the clauses (see Semicolons pages 49 and 50).

Coordinating Conjunctions: for, and, nor, but, or, yet, so (Often referred to as FANBOYS)

For: Explains why or because.
And: Adds more information.
Nor: Adds a negative idea.

But: Adds an exception or contrasting idea.
Or: States a choice.
Yet: States "still" or "even though."
So: States a result or consequence.

The words thrilled Johnny, **but** this was not what he was waiting for, **and** it was not Sam Adams speaking.

Esther Forbes, Johnny Tremain

"Constance says Aunt Arabella was in love once, **but** he died, **and** women like that never get over it."

Sid Fleischman, By the Great Horn Spoon!

Big Toomai prodded Kala Nag spitefully, **for** he was very angry, **but** Little Toomai was too happy to speak.

Rudyard Kipling, The Jungle Book

Punctuate It

Use commas to separate the clauses in a series in each sentence below.

1. Manny played baseball on Monday and he practiced football on Tuesday but he rested on Wednesday.

2. The barking dog chased the cat across the yard but the feline scurried up a tree so the canine gave up and trotted home.

3. Hungry lions roared in their cages and playful monkeys chattered on tree limbs but the tall giraffes grazed quietly.

4. Vanessa wanted to go to the movies but she had homework to finish so she stayed home.

Write It

Write 2 sentences using commas to separate independent clauses in a series. Place a comma followed by a coordinating conjunction after each clause listed.

1. _____

_____

2. _____

_____

Commas Separate Interrupting Words

Use commas to separate interrupting words, phrases, and clauses from the rest of the sentence. Interrupting words "interrupt" the flow of the main sentence. They are nonessential (not essential to the meaning of the sentence), and the sentence can stand alone if the interrupters are removed. Place commas before and after interrupters.

Examples of Common Interrupters: after all, basically speaking, by the way, for example, for instance, for some reason, generally speaking, however, I believe, I guess, in any case, in fact, in my opinion, it seems to me, of course, on one hand

"Gentlemen they are, **most of them**, and the others are too crude for the clever art of the cut-purse."

Sid Fleischman, *By the Great Horn Spoon!*

You don't know much about her or her real disposition, **I suppose,** and there's no guessing how a child like that will turn out.

Lucy Maud Montgomery, *Anne of Green Gables*

"I'll come up in a little while, **in any case,** and tell you what I'm going to do."

Franz Kafka, *Amerika*

Punctuate It

Place commas to separate the interrupting words from the main clause in each sentence below. Each sentence requires two commas.

1. Wynton Marsalis in my opinion is the best trumpet player of all time.

2. He is a talented musician in fact who teaches and composes music.

3. Marsalis I believe was inspired by some of the great horn players of the past.

4. He is known of course throughout the music world.

Write It

Write 2 sentences using commas to separate interrupting words. Place commas before and after the interrupters.

1. _____

_____

2. _____

_____

Commas Separate Nonessential Appositives

Use commas to separate nonessential (not essential) appositives from the rest of the sentence. Appositives are nouns or noun phrases that describe a nearby noun or pronoun. When the nonessential appositive is in the middle of the sentence, place a comma before and after it. When the nonessential appositive is at the end of the sentence, place a comma before it. The sentence should be able to stand alone if the nonessential appositive is removed.

The face of Jim O'Brien, **a Mastodon King and old-time comrade**, caught his eyes.
Jack London, *The Call of the Wild*

At least she was cool in the air-conditioned bedroom she shared with their seven-year-old sister, **Lizzie**, and their grandma.
Suzanne Collins, *Gregor the Overlander*

Mrs. Barney, **my fifth grade teacher**, had turned me on to them.
Jennifer Cervantes, *Tortilla Sun*

Punctuate It
Place commas separating the nonessential appositive phrase from the main clause in each sentence below. Some sentences require more than one comma.

1. John Adams our second president was a leader of the American Revolution.

2. We went to Yosemite a national park in California for our vacation.

3. Kai wanted to buy a new motorcycle one with a fast engine.

4. Mr. Sanchez our geometry teacher taught algebra last year.

Write It
Write 2 sentences using commas to separate nonessential appositive phrases from the rest of the sentence. When the appositive is in the middle of the sentence, place commas before and after the phrase.

1. _____

_____

2. _____

_____

Commas Separate Nonessential Words

Use commas to separate nonessential (not essential) words, phrases, and clauses from the rest of the sentence. The sentence should be able to stand alone if the nonessential words are removed.

Several hundred men, **furred and mittened,** banked around the sled within easy distance.

Jack London, *The Call of the Wild*

"Welcome to the world that contains this lonely pond, **this splendid marsh, unspoiled and wild!**"

E. B. White, *The Trumpet of the Swan*

We set off across the snow fields, **uphill and down,** the way I'd come.

James Lincoln Collier and Christopher Collier, *My Brother Sam Is Dead*

Punctuate It

Place commas to separate the nonessential words from the main clause in each sentence below.

1. Kira who was thirteen liked her job delivering newspapers.

2. Milo climbed the tree slowly and carefully to rescue the cat.

3. The old clock a gift from my mother had stopped working.

4. Sarina ate her dessert a hot fudge sundae after eating dinner.

Write It

Write 2 sentences using commas to separate nonessential words from the rest of the sentence. When the nonessential words are in the middle of the sentence, place commas before and after the words. Each sentence should be able to stand alone if the nonessential words are removed.

1. _____

_____

2. _____

_____

Commas Separate Contrasting Words at the End of Sentences

> Use commas to separate contrasting words, changes in thought, or distinct pauses at the end of sentences.

Marilla went to her room at intervals all through the evening and searched for the brooch, **without find it.**

Lucy Maud Montgomery, *Anne of Green Gables*

They'd never really talked about it, but no one disagreed, **not even Hedge**.

Rick Riordan, *The Heroes of Olympus, The Lost Hero*

They turned to each other, laughing excitedly, talking, **not listening**.

William Golding, *Lord of the Flies*

Punctuate It

Place a comma to separate the contrasting words, changes in thought, or distinct pauses at the end of each sentence below.

1. Everyone wanted to go to the movies even Justin.

2. Liza wanted to be dropped off at 1 p.m. not 2 p.m.

3. Carlos didn't want to go home not now or ever.

4. Josh hoped to attend the science camp this year not next year.

Write It

Write 2 sentences using commas to separate contrasting words, changes in thought, or distinct pauses at the end of each sentence.

1. _____

_____

2. _____

_____

Commas in Compound Sentences

Use commas in compound sentences when using a coordinating conjunction to join the independent clauses or sentences. A compound sentence joins two or more independent clauses. Place commas after the independent clause or clauses. Place a coordinating conjunction after each comma. A semicolon can also be used to join independent clauses (see Semicolons pages 49 and 50).

Coordinating Conjunctions: for, and, nor, but, or, yet, so (Often referred to as FANBOYS)

For: Explains why or because.

And: Adds more information.

Nor: Adds a negative idea.

But: Adds an exception or contrasting idea.

Or: States a choice.

Yet: States "still" or "even though."

So: States a result or consequence.

Laura tried and tried to catch a minnow, **but** she only got the hem of her dress wet.

Laura Ingalls Wilder, *Little House of the Prairie*

I remembered my mother's counsel and my good old master's, **and** I tried to do exactly what he wanted me to do.

Anna Sewell, *Black Beauty*

The words thrilled Johnny, **but** this was not what he was waiting for, **and** it was not Sam Adams speaking.

Esther Forbes, *Johnny Tremain*

Punctuate It

Place a comma to separate the independent clauses in each sentence below.

1. Melanie drives a sports car but her sister drives an old truck.

2. Geno is a baseball pitcher and his brother is a catcher.

3. School was scheduled for half-day so students left at noon.

4. Phil enjoys traveling by car but Mary prefers traveling by plane.

Write It

Write 2 compound sentences using commas to separate the independent clauses. Place a coordinating conjunction (and, but, or, so) after the comma.

1. _____

_____

2. _____

_____

Commas in Complex Sentences

A complex sentence has one independent clause (sentence) and one or more dependent clauses. The dependent clause begins with a subordinating conjunction or a relative pronoun.

Examples of Subordinating Conjunctions: after, although, as, as soon as, because, before, even if, even though, if, now that, once, since, so that, than, though, unless, until, when, whenever, wherever, whether, while

Commonly Used Relative Pronouns: that, which, who, whoever, whose

There are several ways to write a complex sentence.

When the sentence begins with an independent clause and ends with the dependent clause, no comma is needed.

Example: We stayed inside **because the weather was cold**. *No comma needed.*

When the complex sentence begins with a dependent clause, place a comma after the clause.

Example: **Since the weather was cold,** we stayed inside. *Comma needed.*

When Laura and Mary woke, he was gone and everything was empty and lonely.
Laura Ingalls Wilder, *Little House on the Prairie*

As soon as Miles Hendon and the little prince were clear of the mob, they struck down through back lanes and alleys toward the river.
Mark Twain, *The Prince and the Pauper*

When sunshine came again, she was not there.
Nathaniel Hawthorne, *The Scarlet Letter*

Punctuate It

Place a comma after the introductory dependent clause in each sentence below.

1. When Malik finished his lunch he went outside and played tag.

2. Since everyone had gone home Melania left work early.

3. Because it was raining Tisha wore her new raincoat to school.

4. After Kinsley finished her clarinet lesson she packed up her instrument and walked home.

Write It

Write 2 complex sentences beginning with a dependent clause. Place a comma after the dependent clause. End each sentence with an independent clause.

1. _____

_____

2. _____

_____

Commas in Complex Sentences (Cont'd)

Another way to write a complex sentence is to interrupt the independent clause or sentence with a nonessential (not essential) dependent clause. Nonessential clauses add information, but the information is not needed for the main sentence to make sense. Place commas before and after nonessential dependent clauses that interrupt the main clause. Nonessential dependent clauses usually begin with a relative pronoun. The main clause or sentence should be able to stand alone if the non-essential dependent clause is removed.

Relative Pronouns Often Used with Nonessential Clauses: which, who, whose

Mr. Poe took off his top hat, **which had made his head look large and square in the fog,** and stood for a moment, coughing loudly into a white handkerchief.
Lemony Snicket, *A Series of Unfortunate Events: The Bad Beginning*

Pearl, **whose activity of spirit never flagged,** had been at no loss for amusement while her mother talked with the old gatherer of herbs.
Nathaniel Hawthorne, *The Scarlet Letter*

Two security men had rushed to the prime minister, **who was clutching his wrist,** blood dripping out of his hand.
Anthony Horowitz, *Stormbreaker*

Punctuate It
Place commas to separate the nonessential dependent clause from the main clause in each sentence below. Each sentence requires two commas.

1. Lily whose father was a dentist planned on attending medical school.

2. The van which held six passengers was painted bright red.

3. The executive who was very kind let employees leave early.

4. The painting which was sold at the auction had two colors.

Write It
Write 2 complex sentences with a nonessential dependent clause interrupting the independent clause. Use a relative pronoun to begin the dependent clause. Place a comma before and after the dependent clause. The main sentence should be able to stand alone if the dependent clause is removed.

1. _____

_____

2. _____

_____

Commas in Compound-Complex Sentences

Use commas in compound-complex sentences. A compound-complex sentence has two or more independent clauses (sentences) and one or more dependent clauses (sentences that can't stand alone).

Dependent clauses may be essential (required for the main clause to make sense) or nonessential (not required for the main clause to make sense). Use commas to separate nonessential dependent clauses from the independent clause.

To join the independent clauses see Box A below. To add the dependent clauses see Box B below. Pages 41-44 show four different ways to write compound-complex sentences.

BOX A: USE ONE OF THE FOLLOWING TO JOIN INDEPENDENT CLAUSES

USE A COMMA WITH A COORDINATING CONJUNCTION	USE A SEMICOLON WITH A CONJUNCTIVE ADVERB OR USE A SINGLE SEMICOLON
for, and, nor, but, or, yet, so (Often referred to as FANBOYS) **For**: Explains why or because **And**: Adds more information **Nor**: Adds a negative idea **But**: Adds an exception or contrasting idea **Or**: States a choice **Yet**: States "still" or "even though" **So**: States a result or consequence	additionally, also, anyway, as a result, besides, certainly, consequently, conversely, currently, equally, even so, eventually, finally, for example, for instance, furthermore, however, in addition, in fact, instead, likewise, meanwhile, otherwise, similarly, still, subsequently, that is, then, therefore

BOX B: USE ONE OF THE FOLLOWING TO INTRODUCE DEPENDENT CLAUSES

USE A RELATIVE PRONOUN	USE A SUBORDINATING CONJUNCTION
Relative pronouns are used to introduce essential and nonessential dependent clauses. Essential clauses are not separated from the main clause with commas. Nonessential clauses are separated from the main clause using commas. **Common Relative Pronouns**: that, which, who, whose **that**: Use to introduce essential dependent clauses when referring to people, animals, or things. A comma is **not** required. **which**: Use to introduce essential or nonessential dependent clauses when referring to animals or things. **who**: Use to introduce essential or nonessential dependent clauses when referring to people. **whose**: Use to introduce essential or nonessential dependent clauses as a possessive to describe people, animals, or things.	Subordinating conjunctions are used to introduce dependent clauses. When the dependent clause is at the beginning of the sentence, a comma is required. When the dependent clause follows an independent clause, no comma is required. **Common Subordinating Conjunctions**: after, although, as, as if, as soon as, because, before, even if, even so, if, if only, now that, once, since, so that, than, though, unless, until, when, whenever, wherever, whether, while

Commas in Compound-Complex Sentences (Cont'd)

> **Box 1: Begin the sentence with an introductory dependent clause followed by two independent clauses (sentences). Follow the steps below.**
>
> 1. Write the dependent clause beginning with a subordinate conjunction (see Box B on page 41). Place a comma after the dependent clause.
> 2. Add the first independent clause or sentence. Place a comma followed by a coordinating conjunction; or a semicolon followed by a conjunctive adverb; or use a single semicolon after the clause (see Box A on page 41).
> 3. Add the second independent clause or sentence.
>
> Examples:
>
> **Since** it was raining, Tia wore her raincoat, **so** she could stay warm and dry.
>
> **Since** it was raining, Tia wore her raincoat; **therefore**, she stayed warm and dry.
>
> **Since** it was raining, Tia wore her raincoat; she stayed warm and dry.

When we arrived at Gip's little *adobe* home, Gip was on the bumpy tile floor; she lay very still.

Jennifer Cervantes, Tortilla Sun

As quickly as it had come, the wind died, **and** the clearing was quiet again.

John Steinbeck, Of Mice and Men

Punctuate It

Place commas or semicolons in each compound-complex sentence below. Use the instructions from Box 1 above to determine the correct punctuation.

1. When Jay finished his homework he went outside he rode his bike around the neighborhood.
2. Since everyone had gone home Melia left work early so she could beat the rush hour traffic.
3. Because it was raining Tanya wore her new rain boots her feet stayed warm and dry all day.
4. After Libby finished her guitar lesson she went to Briana's house and they finished their school project.

Write It

Use the instructions from Box 1 above to write 2 compound-complex sentences. Begin each sentence with a dependent clause followed by two independent clauses.

1. _____

   _____

2. _____

   _____

Commas in Compound-Complex Sentences (Cont'd)

Box 2: Begin the sentence with two independent clauses (sentences) followed by an essential dependent clause. Follow the steps below.

1. Write the first independent clause or sentence. Place a comma followed by a coordinating conjunction; or a semicolon followed by a conjunctive adverb; or a single semicolon after the clause (see Box A on page 41).

2. Add the second independent clause or sentence (no comma is needed).

3. Add an essential dependent clause using a relative pronoun or a subordinating conjunction (see Box B on page 41).

Examples:

Tia wore her raincoat, **so** she could stay dry **when** she walked home.

Tia wore her raincoat; **subsequently,** she stayed dry **when** she walked home.

Tia wore her raincoat; she stayed dry **when** she walked home.

They were fiercely loyal to Cherry, **and** by the rules of the military the captain of the plane was in charge **until** the mission was over.

Tod Olson, *Lost in the Pacific, 1942*

Heroic music would start to play, **and** Tristan McLean would make his amazing escape, running away in slow motion **while** the mountainside exploded behind him.

Rick Riordan, *The Heroes of Olympus: The Lost Hero*

Punctuate It

Place a comma or semicolon in each compound-complex sentence below. Follow the instructions in Box 2 above to determine the correct punctuation.

1. Marcus ate his lunch he went outside when he was finished.

2. Everyone had gone home therefore Mel left work early because she wanted to beat the rush hour traffic.

3. Trevor attends a military academy he hopes to become an officer when he graduates.

4. Carson played piano meanwhile his brother played the drums while listening to rock music.

Write It

Use the instructions from Box 2 to write 2 compound-complex sentences. Begin each sentence with two independent clauses followed by an essential dependent clause.

1. _____

_____

2. _____

_____

Commas in Compound-Complex Sentences (Cont'd)

> **Box 3:** Begin the sentence with an independent clause (sentence) followed by an essential dependent clause. End the sentence with an independent clause. Follow the steps below.

1. Write the first independent clause or sentence. No comma is needed after the clause.

2. Use a relative pronoun or a subordinating conjunction to add the essential dependent clause (see Box B on page 41).

3. Use a comma followed by a coordinating conjunction; a semicolon followed by a conjunctive adverb; or a single semicolon to add the last independent clause (see Box A on page 41).

Examples:

Tia brought her umbrella **because** it was raining, **so** she could stay dry.

Tia brought her umbrella **because** it was raining; **subsequently,** she stayed dry.

Tia brought her umbrella **because** it was raining; she stayed dry.

I don't mind the thought of work **because** I like to mess around with boats, **but** I want to get out on that ocean so bad I can feel it and taste it and smell it.

Sharon Creech, *The Wanderer*

Little Chuck Little was another member of the population **who** didn't know where his next meal was coming from, **but** he was a born gentleman.

Harper Lee, *To Kill a Mockingbird*

Punctuate It

Place a comma or semicolon in each compound-complex sentence below. Use the instructions from Box 3 to determine correct punctuation.

1. Brian finished his lunch so he went outside since it was a warm day.

2. Everyone had gone home therefore Mel left work early because she wanted to beat the rush hour traffic.

3. Tisha wore her new rain boots her feet stayed warm and dry when she walked home in the rain.

4. Marla finished her clarinet lesson so she went to Briana's house since they had a project to finish.

Write It

Use the instructions from Box 3 to write 2 compound-complex sentences. Begin each sentence with an independent clause followed by an essential dependent clause. End each sentence with an independent clause.

1. _____

_____

2. _____

_____

Commas in Compound-Complex Sentences (Cont'd)

> **Box 4:** Begin the sentence with an independent clause (sentence) followed by a nonessential dependent clause. End the sentence with an independent clause or sentence. Follow the steps below.

1. Write an independent clause or sentence followed by a comma.
2. Add the nonessential (not essential) dependent clause beginning with a relative pronoun (who, which, whose). Place a comma followed by a coordinating conjunction; or a semicolon followed by a conjunctive adverb; or a single semicolon after the clause (see Box A on page 41).
3. Add the last independent clause or sentence.

Examples:

Tia grabbed her raincoat, **which** she wore often, **so** she could stay dry all day.

Tia grabbed her raincoat, **which** she wore often; **therefore,** she stayed dry all day.

Tia grabbed her raincoat, **which** she wore often; **she** stayed dry all day.

"I suppose this cave once had a name," I said to Rontu, **who was as glad to be free as I was**, "but I have never heard of it or heard it spoken about."

Scott O'Dell, *Island of the Blue Dolphins*

His mom only worked part-time then, and his dad, **who'd taught high school science**, was off summers.

Suzanne Collins, *Gregor the Overlander*

Punctuate It

Place a comma or semicolon in each compound-complex sentence below. Use the instructions from Box 4 to determine correct punctuation.

1. Jacob ate his lunch which he gobbled down so he could go outside.
2. The fox slowly approached which I didn't like so I quietly backed away.
3. Misha wore her new rain boots which were bright yellow and her feet stayed warm and dry.
4. Kyla liked Sam who was her best friend they walked to school together every day.

Write It

Use the instructions from Box 4 to write 2 compound-complex sentences. Begin each sentence with an independent clause followed by a nonessential dependent clause. End each sentence with an independent clause or sentence.

1. _____

   _____

2. _____

   _____

Commas in Compound-Complex Sentences (Cont'd)

Punctuate It

Place commas or semicolons in the compound-complex sentences below. Some sentences require two punctuation marks.

1. The famous movie star signed autographs and she smiled for the camera as the photographer took several pictures.
2. When the Corvette sped around the corner the driver hit the brakes and the sports car came to a sudden stop.
3. Because it snowed all day Susan stayed home so she decided to watch a movie.
4. Rebecca wanted to ride her new bike however her mother said she would have to wait because it was too cold.
5. Since their team won the players celebrated they went out for pizza.
6. When Maria returned home she headed straight to the kitchen because she was hungry.
7. The teacher held up an old object which looked like a plate and she asked the class to examine it.
8. Mira traveled by boat around the world which was her life-long dream it took fifty days.
9. When she reached the Panama Canal it was amazing to see how the boats were lifted up and down the canal in fact even huge cargo ships could pass through.

Write It

Use what you have learned to write a paragraph with compound, complex, and compound-complex sentences.

_____

_____

_____

_____

_____

_____

_____

Commas Separate Dialogue from the Dialogue Tag

Use commas to separate dialogue (the exact words spoken) from the dialogue tag. The dialogue tag states who is speaking. The tag may be placed in the beginning, middle, or end of the sentence.

Examples: "I have to go home now," Andy announced.

  (The Dialogue)   (The Dialogue Tag)

"I have to go now," Paulo said, "before it gets too late.

  (The Dialogue)   (The Dialogue Tag)   (The Dialogue)

"Your mother and I got you up," said Pod, "to tell you about upstairs."

Mary Norton, *The Borrowers*

Miss Thomas said, "There's lots wrong, but not with that car."

Christopher Paul Curtis, *Bud, Not Buddy*

"It's a shame about Sam," Mr. Heron said.

James Lincoln Collier and Christopher Collier, *My Brother Sam is Dead*

Punctuate It

Place commas separating the dialogue from the dialogue tag in each sentence below.

1. "Jamie is ready to go home now" Mia announced.

2. Ed asked "May I have a ride to school?"

3. "Most volunteers" stated Jamal "like to work in the morning."

4. "We will leave for the play at noon" announced Martina.

Write It

Write 2 sentences using commas to separate the dialogue from the dialogue tag.

1. _____

_____

2. _____

_____

Pro Tip: Use Commas to Extend the Dialogue Tag

Extend the dialogue tag by adding descriptive phrases and clauses after the tag. Use a comma to separate the dialogue tag from the descriptive words. Try adding prepositional phrases, participial phrases, and dependent clauses after the tag (see the Table of Contents to refer to these types of sentences). Notice in the examples below how the professional authors extend the dialogue tag by adding descriptive phrases and clauses.

"Wake up, Centipede," whispered James, **giving him a gentle dig in the stomach.**
Roald Dahl, *James and the Giant Peach*

"He'll be eaten if we don't do something," said Thorin, **for there were howls all around them now, getting nearer and nearer.**
J. R. R. Tolkien, *The Hobbit*

"I suppose this cave once had a name," I said to Rontu, **who was as glad to be free as I was**, "but I have never heard of it or heard it spoken about."
Scott O'Dell, *Island of the Blue Dolphins*

Punctuate It
Place commas separating the dialogue tag from the descriptive words in each sentence below.

1. "I have to study," complained Chen opening his math book.

2. "Let's hurry," said Keenan looking down at his watch, "so we can catch the next bus."

3. "Everyone is going to the dance tonight," Hazel explained hoping her mother would let her go.

4. "I hope I win the spelling bee," said Omar crossing his fingers for good luck.

Write It
Write 2 sentences with dialogue. Extend the dialogue tag by adding a descriptive phrase or clause.

1. _____

_____

2. _____

_____

Semicolons to Join Independent Clauses

Use semicolons to join related independent clauses or sentences. Place the semicolon after each independent clause. Place one space after the semicolon. The first word after the semicolon begins with a lower case letter unless it's a proper noun or proper adjective. Sentences with two or more independent clauses may contain more than one semicolon, or they may contain a combination of semicolons with a comma and coordinating conjunction as shown in the last example below written by Walter Farley.

Almost every day the horses traveled as far as they could; almost every night Pa and Ma made camp in a new place.

Laura Ingalls Wilder, *Little House on the Prairie*

"We do not drink where the monkeys drink; we do not go where the monkeys go; we do not hunt where they hunt; we do not die where they die."

Rudyard Kipling, *The Jungle Book*

He could see the stallion was nervous; the horse had learned to trust him, **but** his natural instincts still warned him against the others.

Walter Farley, *The Black Stallion*

Punctuate It

Place semicolons to separate the independent clauses in each compound sentence below. One sentence requires more than one semicolon.

1. The train left late it arrived early.

2. Cora played violin her sister played piano her brother played drums.

3. School begins in August it ends in June.

4. Manuela baked chocolate cupcakes her mother iced them.

Write It

Write 2 compound sentences using a semicolon to join related independent clauses. Place the semicolon after the first clause. Place one space after the semicolon.

1. _____

_____

2. _____

_____

Semicolons to Join Independent Clauses with Conjunctive Adverbs

> Use semicolons with conjunctive adverbs to join related independent clauses. Conjunctive adverbs are used like conjunctions to transition between sentences. Place the semicolon before the conjunctive adverb and a comma after the adverb.
>
> Examples of Conjunctive Adverbs: additionally, almost, also, anyway, as a result, besides, certainly, consequently, conversely, currently, equally, eventually, finally, furthermore, however, in addition, in fact, indeed, instead, likewise, meanwhile, nevertheless, otherwise, similarly, still, subsequently, that is, then, therefore

The Rat was a self-sufficing sort of animal, rooted to the land, and, whoever went, he stayed; **still,** he could not help noticing what was in the air, and feeling some of its influence in his bones.

Kenneth Grahame, *The Wind in the Willows*

Others attempted to hop over the gullies to the forest to bypass the hole; **however,** we knew from much experience that they would not make it.

Mildred D. Taylor, *Roll of Thunder, Hear My Cry*

Robinson proposed that they should spend the night here, since they were all very tired and would be able to start all the earlier in the morning; **besides,** they would scarcely find a cheaper and more suitable place to spend the night before complete darkness fell.

Franz Kafka, *Amerika*

Punctuate It

Place a semicolon before the conjunctive adverb in each compound sentence below. Place a comma after the conjunctive adverb.

1. The kitten chased the mouse however the mouse escaped.

2. Alyssa loved to play tennis therefore she played every day.

3. Shira didn't eat breakfast as a result she had no energy.

4. Marty was a quick starter however he was a slow finisher.

Write It

Write 2 compound sentences using a semicolon followed by a conjunctive adverb to join the independent clauses. Place a comma after the adverb.

1. _____

_____

2. _____

_____

Semicolons to Eliminate Sentence Confusion

Semicolons can be used (in place of commas) to separate groups of words in a list or series to help eliminate sentence confusion. For example, in the sentence below it may be confusing using commas to separate the series, so semicolons can be used to separate the lists to make the sentence easier to understand.

Confusing: This year we will visit Santa Fe, New Mexico, New York, New York, New Orleans, Louisiana, and Newtown, Virginia.

Better: This year we will visit Santa Fe, New Mexico; New York, New York; New Orleans, Louisiana; and Newtown, Virginia.

He could see the whole front of Toad Hall, glowing in the evening sunshine, the pigeons settling by twos and threes along the straight line of the roof; the garden, a blaze of flowers; the creek that led up to the boat-house, the little wooden bridge that crossed it; all tranquil, uninhabited, apparently waiting for his return.

Kenneth Grahame, *The Wind in the Willows*

Rounding out their worldly possessions were the following items: eight inflatable life vests; two sheath knives, a pen knife, and a pair of pliers; eighteen flares and a Very pistol to fire them; two .45 caliber pistols and some ammunition; three sets of aluminum oars; two collapsible rubber bailing buckets; two hand pumps and three patch kits to keep the rafts inflated; a few pencils; and, finally, a pocket compass and a map of the Pacific.

Tod Olson, *Lost in the Pacific, 1942*

The classes were the same: language and communications; commerce and industry; science and technology; civil procedures and government.

Lois Lowry, *The Giver*

Punctuate It
Replace two of the commas with semicolons to help eliminate confusion in the sentence below.

Edwin's walls were decorated with famous athletes like: baseball players Babe Ruth, Jackie Robinson, and Hank Aaron, football players Joe Montana, Bart Star, and Tony Romo, and basketball players Michael Jordan, Stephen Curry, Kevin Durant, and LeBron James.

Write It
Write one sentence with groups of words in a series. Use semicolons to separate the groups of words in the series to help eliminate sentence confusion.

_____

_____

_____

Colons Introduce Lists

Use colons after main clauses or sentences to introduce a list that follows. Place one space after the colon. The first word in the list begins with a lower case letter unless it's a proper noun or proper adjective. Place a comma after each word in the list. Place a coordinate conjunction (and, or, but) after the last comma.

Every part of him was defined: small, strong hands, slender arms, a thin and bony nose.

John Steinbeck, *Of Mice and Men*

Daisy Babcock, working with Fran Brodie, had planned a decorative scheme based on the Pickax High School colors: gray, black, and gold.

Lilian Jackson Braun, *The Cat Who Had 60 Whiskers*

It's like a sixth sense: a combination of hearing, sight, and smell.

Jules Verne, *Around the World in Eighty Days*

Punctuate It

Place a colon to separate the main clause from the list in each sentence below.

1. Kendra bought everything needed to make the cake flour, sugar, vanilla, eggs, butter, and salt.

2. Bradley made a list of the cities he would visit as follows Paris, London, New York, Tokyo, and Moscow.

3. The colorful bouquet of flowers included red roses, yellow daffodils, pink carnations, and white lilies.

4. Kim and Ken considered the following names for their baby Kayden, Kenzley, Katelynn, or Kendra.

Write It

Write 2 sentences using a colon after a main clause that introduces a list. After the colon, add the list. Place commas between the words listed.

1. _____

_____

2. _____

_____

Colons After Clauses that Introduce More Information

Use colons after main clauses or sentences that introduce more information. The words that follow the colon emphasize the information in the clause. Place one space after the colon. The first word after the colon usually begins with a lower case letter unless it's a proper noun or proper adjective.

"If I am ever made to get married," thought the Wart, who had doubts on this subject, "I will marry a girl like this: a kind of golden vixen."
T. H. White, *The Sword in the Stone*

There were three rules in their private game: except for seasonings they must not use anything in the Mundys' cupboards or refrigerator for their meal, they could not add any money of their own to the sum Mrs. Mundy had given them, and they must spend every penny of this sum.
Beverly Cleary, *Jean and Johnny*

He was glad for one thing: the rope was off his neck.
Jack London, *The Call of the Wild*

Punctuate It
Place a colon after the main clause that introduces more information in each sentence below.

1. Tami crossed the finish line in record time one minute even.

2. No one heard it or saw it coming a swift moving avalanche.

3. Henry didn't want anyone to know his secret he had lied.

4. Marsha couldn't believe what she had found a fifty-dollar bill.

Write It
Write 2 sentences using colons after a main clause that introduces more information. Place a colon after each clause followed by the words that add more information.

1. _____

_____

2. _____

_____

Colons After Clauses that Introduce Formal Quotes

Use colons after main clauses or sentences that introduce formal quotes. Place the colon directly after the introductory clause. Place one space after the colon followed by the quote. Remember to place quotation marks around the quote.

Example: In President John F. Kennedy's most famous speech, he said: "My fellow Americans, ask not what your country can do for you, ask what you can do for your country."

Punctuate It

Place a colon after the main clause that introduces the formal quote.

1. Many soldiers carry the words of Mark Twain with them into battle "Courage is resistance to fear, mastery of fear, not absence of fear."

2. Albert Einstein, the famous physicist, once stated "If you are out to describe the truth, leave elegance to the tailor."

3. Sir Isaac Newton's third law of motion states "For every action, there is an equal and opposite reaction."

4. Our first president, George Washington, once said "The Constitution is the guide which I never will abandon."

Write It

Use a book, magazine, or the internet to find a formal quote. Write 2 sentences beginning with a statement that introduces the quote followed by a colon. Use quotation marks around the exact words quoted from the source or text.

1. _____

_____

2. _____

_____

Colons After Greetings in Business Letters

> **Use a colon after the greeting in a business letter.**
>
> Dear Sir: Dear Principal Brock: Dear President Johnson:

Punctuate It
Place colons after the greetings below.

1. Dear Mrs. Jones **3.** To Whom It May Concern **5.** Dear Sir

2. Dear Rev. Roberts **4.** Dear Dr. Singh **6.** Dear Ms. Li

Colons Separate Hours and Minutes in Clock Time

> **Use a colon to separate the hours and the minutes in clock time.**
>
> **Example:** Tamara left at 7:30 a.m. to catch the school bus.

At 3:32 precisely, I noticed Kaitlyn striding confidently past the Wok House.
John Green, *The Fault in Our Stars*

I blinked at the clock on my nightstand: 6:45.
Jennifer Cervantes, *Tortilla Sun*

School begins every morning at 8:30 a.m.

Punctuate It
Place colons between the hours and minutes.

1. 9 30 a.m. **2.** 12 30 p.m. **3.** 8 00 a.m. **4.** 10 00 p.m.

Write It
Write 2 sentences using clock time in each sentence.

1. _____

_____

2. _____

_____

Quotation Marks Around Dialogue

Use quotation marks around dialogue (the exact words spoken). Place the dialogue punctuation inside the quotation marks. Use interesting dialogue tags.

Example: "It's time to go home!" announced Dorothy.

Examples of Interesting Dialogue Tags: agreed, announced, argued, asked, begged, blurted, boasted, chanted, claimed, commented, cried, demanded, explained, growled, hollered, howled, insisted, joked, noted, objected, ordered, pleaded, prayed, promised, questioned, quoted, repeated, remarked, replied, scolded, screamed, shouted, sighed, squealed, stammered, stated, stuttered, wailed, warned, whimpered, whispered, yelled

Steady Eddie said, "Don't thank me until you've been through a couple of hours of blowing scales. We'll see if you're still grateful then."

Christopher Paul Curtis, *Bud, Not Buddy*

"What do you want with that?" growled the carter, as he cracked his whip and was moving on.

Anna Sewell, *Black Beauty*

"Oh, Pod," wailed Homily, "I should have never have let you go."

Mary Norton, *The Borrowers*

Punctuate It

Place quotation marks around the dialogue in each sentence below.

1. Have a nice day, Manny shouted, see you tomorrow.

2. Elise asked, Does anyone want to play basketball at recess?

3. The teacher announced, Everyone passed the math test!

4. What time does the soccer game start? Lisa asked.

Write It

Write 2 sentences using quotation marks around dialogue. Place quotation marks around the exact words spoken and the dialogue punctuation. Use interesting dialogue tags.

1. _____

_____

2. _____

_____

Single Quotation Marks Around a Quote Within a Quote

Use single quotation marks around a quote within a quote. This rule applies when writing dialogue, and the speaker quotes words that someone else has stated. Place single quotation marks around the exact words quoted within the dialogue. Place double quotation marks around the entire quote.

When the words that are quoted are at the end of the sentence, and the sentence ends with a period, place the single quotation mark and the double quotation mark after the period.

Example: Mom announced, "Dad said, 'clean your room today.'"

Question marks and exclamation points can go inside or outside the single quotation mark, depending on whether the punctuation is part of the original quote.

Examples: Sarah inquired, "Did dad ask, 'Are you going to the dance?'"

Dad asked, "Did you hear your mom say, 'clean your room'?"

"I don't know what you mean when you say 'the whole world' or 'generations before him.' I thought there was only us."

Lois Lowry, *The Giver*

"When I say 'salutations,' it's just my fancy way of saying hello or good morning."

E. B. White, *Charlotte's Web*

"'Barnacles on the container ship of consciousness,'" I said, quoting AIA.

John Green, *The Fault in Our Stars*

Punctuate It

Place single quotation marks around the exact words quoted within the dialogue in each sentence below.

1. "I heard Dad say, wash the car," Dion announced.

2. "Mario said, meet at ten sharp!" Shannon yelled.

3. "Did Shirley say, it cost five dollars?" asked Tim.

4. "Kyle said, put two cookies in his lunch," Josie said.

Write It

Write 2 sentences with a quote within a quote. Use single quotation marks around the exact words quoted within the dialogue. Place double quotation marks around the entire dialogue.

1. _____

_____

2. _____

_____

Quotation Marks Around Words Quoted

Use quotation marks around words that are quoted from a source or text. Place quotation marks before and after the exact words quoted. Periods and commas are placed inside the quotation marks. Question marks and exclamation points can go inside or outside the quotation marks, depending on whether the punctuation is part of the original quote.

Examples: The President stated, "We will keep our country safe!"

Did the President say, "We will keep our country safe"?

One way to introduce the quote is to write a sentence using the relative pronoun "that" right before the quoted words. No comma is required.

Example: *Spirit Magazine* stated **that** "Brazil was one of the most interesting countries in the world to visit."

You can also introduce the quote using a phrase. Place a comma after the phrase.

Example: According to *Healthy Lifestyle Magazine*, "Walking for thirty minutes a day is the easiest way to exercise."

Punctuate It

Place quotation marks around the exact words quoted in each sentence below.

1. According to *Facts.com*, Istanbul, Turkey, is the only city in the world with land on two continents.

2. *Life Magazine* recently reported that Elizabeth Taylor had appeared on the cover more than any other celebrity.

3. A 2015 NASA study reported an increase in Antarctic snow is adding enough ice to the continent to outweigh losses in thinning glaciers.

4. April's *Amazing Animals Magazine* reported that the fastest land animal, the cheetah, was clocked at seventy miles per hour.

Write It

Use a book, magazine, or the internet to find a fact to quote. Write 2 sentences using quotation marks around the words that are quoted from the source. Place quotation marks before and after the exact words quoted.

1. _____

_____

2. _____

_____

Quotation Marks Around Slang Words

Use quotation marks around slang words and expressions. Slang words include vocabulary used informally by specific groups of people and those individuals who live in specific geographical regions. Slang words often have a unique meaning understood by the speaker or the group.

Examples of Slang Words: airhead, bad, bogus, bonkers, boo-hoo, bummer, chill, clutch, cool, ditsy, do over, dork, drag, dude, geek, glitzy grubby, hip, hunk, jock, meltdown, okie-dokie, split, toast, weirdo, wild

Example: The toddler had a "meltdown." *"Meltdown" means breakdown or tantrum.*

It was like someone had wiped his memory, and she was stuck in the worst "do over" of all time.

Rick Riordan, *The Heroes of Olympus: The Lost Hero*

We've been trying to use the sextant for navigation, since our GPS is "toast," as Uncle Dock says.

Sharon Creech, *The Wanderer*

She had a thick Spanish accent, and had on her "painted face," as Mom would have said.

Jennifer Cervantes, Tortilla Sun

Punctuate It
Place quotation marks around the slang word in each sentence below.

1. Janelle thought it was a bummer that the party was cancelled.

2. Nina liked her costume and glitzy jewelry.

3. Taj bought a cool looking red sports car.

4. Aunt Barb likes to say okie-dokie when she means okay.

Write It
Write 2 sentences using a slang word in each sentence. Place quotation marks around the slang word.

1. _____

_____

2. _____

_____

Quotation Marks Around Titles of Shorter Works of Writing

> Use quotation marks around titles of shorter works of writing such as songs, poems, articles, short stories, and chapter titles. Longer works of writing require underlining or italicizing (see Underline or Italicize Titles page 62).

When he played "Summertime" from *Porgy and Bess*, the people of Philadelphia felt that it was the most thrilling music they had ever heard.

E. B. White, *The Trumpet of the Swan*

Qwilleran recited Robert Burns's poem "A Man's a Man for All That."

Lilian Jackson Braun, *The Cat Who Had 60 Whiskers*

"Only A Wisp of Hope," reported the *Lewiston Tribune* in Idaho.

Tod Olson, *Lost in the Pacific, 1942*

Punctuate It

Place quotation marks around the titles of the shorter works of writing in each sentence below.

1. Joni's favorite poem is Phenomenal Woman by Maya Angelou.

2. The short story Rapunzel is a well-known children's fairy tale.

3. The Beatles released the song Hey Jude in 1968.

4. The Road Not Taken is Robert Frost's most famous poem.

Write It

Write 2 sentences using quotation marks around the title of a poem, song, short story, article, or chapter title.

1. _____

_____

2. _____

_____

Pro Tip: Use Quotation Marks with Sound Words in Dialogue

When a person or animal makes a sound, write it as dialogue. Place quotation marks around the sound words. Use interesting dialogue tags when writing sounds words. Non-dialogue sounds can be italicized (see Italicize Sound Words page 66).

Examples of Dialogue Tags for Humans Making Sounds: bawled, bellowed, cheered, cried, groaned, grumbled, grunted, hummed, moaned, mumbled, panted, roared, screamed, screeched, shrieked, sobbed, squealed, wailed, whimpered, whined

Examples of Dialogue Tags for Animals Making Sounds: barked, cheeped, chirped, croaked, crowed, growled, hissed, hooted, howled, neighed, panted, roared, snarled, snorted, squeaked, squealed, squawked, yapped, yelped

"Vroom, vroom!" one of the Earthborn bellowed, and the others took up the chant, each moving his six hands as though driving a car, as if it were some kind of weird religious ritual.

Rick Riordan, *The Heroes of Olympus: The Lost Hero*

"Geurgh!" Mr. Grin gestured and Alex followed him back down the corridor and out of the house.

Anthony Horowitz, *Stormbreaker*

"Hush, hush! Tu-whoo, tu-whoo," said the Owl.

C. S. Lewis, *The Silver Chair*

Punctuate It

Place quotation marks around the sound words in each sentence below.

1. The tiny puppy barked, Arff, arff, arff.

2. When the mouse jumped on Sara's book, she screeched, Ahhhhhh!

3. The squirrel scurried up the tree squealing, Eeek, eek, eek.

4. Oink, oink, oink, the hungry pig snorted.

Write It

Write 2 sentences with dialogue using quotation marks around sound words. Use interesting dialogue tags.

1. _____

_____

2. _____

_____

Underline or Italicize Titles of Longer Works of Writing

Underline or italicize titles of longer works of writing such as books, plays, movies, CDs, DVDs, or magazine titles used in sentences. Shorter works of writing require quotation marks around the title (see Quotation Marks Around Titles of Shorter Works of Writing page 60).

Examples: My favorite book is <u>The Wizard of Oz</u>. Or

My favorite book is *The Wizard of Oz.*

The morning after this saying, the engagement of Gordon Lowther to Miss Lockhart, the science teacher, was announced in *The Scotsman*.

Muriel Spark, *The Prime of Miss Jean Brodie*

"Act Three of *The Marvelous Marriage* by Al Funcoot is about to begin!" a man with a clipboard shouted.

Lemony Snicket, *A Series of Unfortunate Events: The Bad Beginning*

"Only A Wisp of Hope," reported the *Lewiston Tribune* in Idaho.

Tod Olson, *Lost in the Pacific, 1942*

Punctuate It
Underline the titles of longer works of writing in each sentence below.

1. Romeo and Juliet is my favorite Shakespeare play.

2. The children's book Charlotte's Webb is a wonderful story.

3. The movie Jurassic Park was filmed in Hawaii.

4. The Lion King is a popular children's movie.

Write It
Write 2 sentences with a book, magazine, movie, CD, or play title. Underline or italicize the title.

1. _____

_____

2. _____

_____

Underline or Italicize Names of Vehicles, Paintings, and Sculptures

> Underline or italicize specific names given to vehicles such as ships, trains, and spacecraft.
>
> **Examples:** The <u>Orient Express</u> has transported passengers since 1883.
>
> The *Orient Express* has transported passengers since 1883.
>
> Underline or italicize the names of paintings and sculptures.
>
> **Examples:** The most famous painting in the world is the <u>Mona Lisa</u>.
>
> The most famous painting in the world is the *Mona Lisa*.

The *Hispaniola* rolled steadily, dipping her bowsprit now and then with a whiff of spray.

Robert Louis Stevenson, *Treasure Island*

In the hall was hung a reproduction of Botticelli's *Primavera* which means The Birth of Spring.

Muriel Spark, *The Prime of Miss Jean Brodie*

For each ship, the *Dartmouth*, the *Eleanor*, and the brig, the *Beaver*, we will need thirty stout, honest, fearless men and boys.

Esther Forbes, *Johnny Tremain*

Punctuate It
Underline the vehicle, painting, or sculpture name in each sentence below.

1. My grandfather traveled on the Queen Mary passenger ship.

2. Vincent van Gogh painted Starry Night in 1889.

3. The space shuttle Discovery completed thirty-nine flights.

4. Leonardo da Vinci began painting the Mona Lisa in 1503.

Write It
Write 2 sentences with the specific name of a vehicle, painting, or sculpture. Underline or italicize the name.

1. _____

_____

2. _____

_____

Italicize Internal Thoughts of Characters

Italicize the internal thoughts of characters. Internal thoughts express what the character is thinking or wondering. Internal thought dialogue tags can be used to let the reader know that the words are internal thoughts. Some authors write internal thoughts as dialogue (see Quotation Marks page 56).

Examples of Internal Thought Dialogue Tags: considered, decided, hoped, I told myself, memorized, pondered, prayed, remembered, think, thought, a voice in his head whispered, wished, wondered

I remembered her words the night she spoke to Nana back in California: *Do you think she'll forgive me?*

Jennifer Cervantes, *Tortilla Sun*

Something else, he told himself, *something stranger than ever this time, is about to happen to me again soon.*

Roald Dahl, *James and the Giant Peach*

He would know which way to go, I told myself. *He would know*.

Lois Lowry, *The Giver*

She just had time to think: *This would be a stupid way to die*.

Rick Riordan, *The Heroes of Olympus: The Lost Hero*

Write It

Write 2 sentences italicizing the internal thoughts of a character. Use an internal thought dialogue tag.

1. _____

   _____

2. _____

   _____

Italicize Words and Phrases for Emphasis

Italicize words and phrases for emphasis. Notice how the authors below italicize action words, words for emphasis, and non-English words.

"But for heaven's sake—you're *wizards!* You can do *magic!* Surely you can sort out—well—*anything!*"

J. K. Rowling, *Harry Potter and the Half-Blood Prince*

Then he leaned toward me and said with a warm smile, *"Bienvenida.* Welcome."

Jennifer Cervantes, *Tortilla Sun*

Wilbur burst into tears. "I don't *want* to die," he moaned.

E. B. White, *Charlotte's Web*

Punctuate It
Complete each sentence below by adding an appropriate word for emphasis. Italicize each word by tilting the letters to the right.

1. Chip told Cathy he _____ to win the golf tournament.

2. Sophia found _____ dollars at the bottom of her purse!

3. "You did _____?" Francis asked, staring at her friend.

4. Lorraine couldn't believe her eyes when she saw a _____!

Write It
Write 2 sentences italicizing a word or words for emphasis.

1. _____

_____

2. _____

_____

Pro Tip: Italicize Non-Dialogue Sound Words for Emphasis

Italicize non-dialogue sound words (onomatopoeia words) for emphasis. Notice in the passages below how the authors use italicizing, exclamation points, repetition, and capitalization to vary the emphasis placed on the sound words.

Examples of Non-Dialogue Sound Words: bang, boom, buzz, clang, clank, clatter, click, clink, cluck, crash, creak, hiss, hum, jingle, pop, pow, purr, rattle, ring, rumble, screech, sizzle, slurp, snap, splat, swish, toot, thud, thump, whack, wham, whir, whiz

Snap. A bright orange light sizzled to life—an emergency flare—and Leo was temporarily blinded.

CRASH! The stained glass ceiling splintered in a ruin of multicolored shards, and Festus the bronze dragon dropped into the department store.

The dragon clicked. Long *creak.* Two short *clicks. Creak. Creak.*

Bang! Jason found himself flat on his back.

Rick Riordan, *The Heroes of Olympus: The Lost Hero*

I slammed my forehead right into the top of the doorframe. *Wham!*

Jennifer Cervantes, *Tortilla Sun*

Punctuate It

Complete each sentence below by adding a sound word for emphasis. Italicize each sound word by tilting the letters to the right.

1. Aliyah tiptoed across the _____ wooden floor.

2. Lorenzo jumped off the slide and landed with a _____!

3. _____! A loud animal noise could be heard from the forest.

4. Liam stuck a pin in the balloon and it burst with a _____!

Write It

Write two sentences italicizing sound words for emphasis. Try using lower case letters, capital letters, exclamation points, and repetition to emphasize the sound words.

1. _____

_____

2. _____

_____

Parentheses Around Words to Add Information or Clarify

Use parentheses in sentences around information that explains or clarifies. The sentence should be able to stand alone if the information in the parentheses is removed.

The first letter of the first word in the parentheses is lowercase unless it's a proper noun or proper adjective. When the information is placed at the end of the sentence, place the information inside the period.

Example: Abraham Lincoln was our sixteenth president (1861-1865).

When I was almost six and Jem was nearly ten, our summertime boundaries (within calling distance of Calpurnia) were Mrs. Henry Lafayette Dubose's house two doors to the north of us, and the Radley Place three doors to the south.
Harper Lee, *To Kill a Mockingbird*

There was a little cave (a wholesome one with a pebbly floor) at the foot of the steps and near the end of the stony ford.
J. R. R. Tolkien, *The Hobbit*

"Say yes," all five faces (big and little) mouthed at him.
Esther Forbes, *Johnny Tremain*

Punctuate It

Place parentheses around the information that explains or clarifies in each sentence below.

1. The sail fish not the shark is the fastest sea animal.

2. George Washington 1732-1799 was America's first president.

3. The White House a huge mansion took eight years to build.

4. The Space Shuttle Discovery first launched in 1984 was the third space shuttle orbiter to fly in space.

Write It

Write 2 sentences using parentheses around information that explains or clarifies.

1. _____

_____

2. _____

_____

Parentheses Around Numbers or Letters When Listing

> Use parentheses around numbers or letters when listing information. Place a comma after each listed item. Place a coordinating conjunction (and, or, but) after the last comma.

Peter Van Houten was the only person I'd ever come across who seemed to (a) understand what it's like to be dying, and (b) not have died.

John Green, *The Fault in Our Stars*

What I mean is: It's pretty well established that Koko (a) knows what's going to happen. Does he also (b) *make things happen?*

Lilian Jackson Braun, *The Cat Who Had 60 Whiskers*

Remember to buy (1) milk, (2) bread, (3) butter, and (4) eggs.

Punctuate It

Place parentheses around the numbers or letters in each sentence below.

1. Brenda agreed to pick up supplies for 1 Kendra, 2 Maryanne, 3 Sybil, and 4 Tara.

2. Lily counted her change and found a two quarters, b three dimes, c five nickels, and d ten pennies.

3. The painter purchased the following supplies a one gallon of paint, b two rollers, c one paint tarp, and d three brushes.

4. I can think of three ways to be healthier 1 eat nutritious foods, 2 drink twenty ounces of water daily, and 3 exercise four days a week.

Write It

Write 2 sentences using numbers or letters to list words or phrases. Place parentheses around the numbers or letters.

1. _____

   _____

2. _____

   _____

Brackets to Insert Letters or Words in Quotes

Use brackets to insert your own letters or words into quoted materials to help clarify the meaning of the quote. Brackets are placed before and after the inserted letters or words to show that they are not part of the original quote.

Every Friend to his Country, to Himself, and to Posterity, is now called upon to meet at Faneuil Hall, at nine o'clock this day [that, of course, is tomorrow Monday], at which time the bells will ring to make united and successful resistance to this last, worst and most destructive measure of Administration...Boston, Nov. 29, 1773.
Esther Forbes, *Johnny Tremain*

Grandma often said, "You [her grandchildren] are my little sweet peas."

"And it is I, Raksha [The Demon], who answer."
Rudyard Kipling, *The Jungle Book*

Write It

Use the internet or other source to find a quote. Write 2 sentences with a quote. Insert your own letters or words into the quote. Place brackets around the information you added.

1. _____

_____

_____

_____

2. _____

_____

_____

_____

Ellipses Show a Drop Off of Speech

Use the ellipsis (plural ellipses) in dialogue to indicate a trailing off or drop off of speech. While the ellipsis can be written several ways, the easiest way is to write three consecutive periods directly after the last letter of the word that is trailing off. When the ellipsis is at the end of a sentence, write the end punctuation directly after the ellipsis. Do not place a comma after ellipses in dialogue.

"Once they've got the habit and the taste of blood..." Again he shook his head sadly.

Jack London, *White Fang*

"What do you...I'm afraid I...What?" blustered the Prime Minister.

J. K. Rowling, *Harry Potter and the Half-Blood Prince*

"Don't know, kid..." The pilot's words were a hiss, barely audible.

Gary Paulsen, *Hatchet*

Punctuate It

Place an ellipsis after the drop off of speech in each sentence below.

1. "Why did this have to happen? Why did   ?"

2. "It won't work. I can't hold   " Jessica screamed.

3. "I am not a thief. I am not   " cried Joel.

4. "Mom, I need school supplies, but   " Enzo hesitated.

Write It

Write 2 sentences using ellipses to indicate a trailing off or drop off of speech.

1. _____

_____

2. _____

_____

Ellipses to Indicate a Quote Has Been Shortened

Use the ellipsis (plural: ellipses) to indicate that words have been removed from a quote. Removing words from a quote is sometimes done to eliminate writing the entire quote. The ellipsis replace the words that have been removed. Ellipsis are made by writing three consecutive periods after the last word you are writing from the quote. Quotation marks are placed around the words quoted and the ellipsis. Place a period after the ellipsis at the end of the sentence.

Example: In Martin Luther King Jr.'s "I Have a Dream" speech, five paragraphs begin with these famous words: "I have a dream that one day...."

Write It

Use the quote below from the novel *A Tale of Two Cities* written by Charles Dickens. Write a sentence to introduce the quote followed by a colon. Then write part of the speech followed by ellipsis to indicate that words have been removed. Place quotation marks around the words quoted and the ellipsis.

It was the best of times, it was the worst of times, it was the age of wisdom, it was the age of foolishness, it was the epoch of belief, it was the epoch of incredulity, it was the season of Light, it was the season of Darkness, it was the spring of hope, it was the winter of despair, we had everything before us, we had nothing before us, we were all going direct to Heaven, we were all going direct the other way—in short, the period was so far like the present period, that some of its noisiest authorities insisted on its being received, for good or for evil, in the superlative degree of comparison only.

_____

_____

_____

_____

_____

_____

_____

Dashes to Emphasize Words

Use dashes to emphasize words in a clause or sentence. The dash is about double the length of a hyphen. Place the dash before and after the emphasized words when they are in the middle of the sentence and before the emphasized words at the end of the sentence. There is no space between the dashes and the rest of the sentence. The sentence should be able to stand alone if the words in the dashes are removed.

If I had the courage—**and I haven't**—we'd take off down this road and never come back.

Michael Morpurgo, *War Horse*

It was silly to feel so confused, just because she was walking down the hall with a boy—**two boys**—but Jean could not help it.

Beverly Cleary, *Jean and Johnny*

"There is an old war between this lame tiger and myself—**a very old war, and**— I have won."

Rudyard Kipling, *The Jungle Book*

Punctuate It
Place dashes to separate the words that emphasize a point in each sentence below. Some of the sentences require two dashes.

1. The prince had no idea not a hint that he had been tricked.

2. All children naughty or nice will receive a gift.

3. Jordan couldn't believe his luck his bad luck.

4. It took time a very long time to reach the top of Mt. Everest.

Write It
Write 2 sentences using dashes to separate words that emphasize a point. Each sentence should be able to stand alone if the words in the dashes are removed.

1. _____

_____

2. _____

_____

Dashes with an Interruption in Speech or Sudden Change of Thought

Use dashes to indicate an abrupt interruption in speech or sudden change of thought in a clause or sentence. Place the dash after the words that are interrupted. If the words that are interrupted are in the **middle of the** sentence, place dashes before and after the words. There is no space between the dash and the rest of the sentence.

Luxa's eyes widened, and a strange expression crossed her face. "Vikus, you do not think he—"

Suzanne Collins, *Gregor the Overlander*

He knew lots of girls—**wouldn't you just know**—and he spent a lot of time talking to them in the halls.

Beverly Cleary, *Jean and Johnny*

"As talented as you—" Blunt cut in.

Anthony Horowitz, *Stormbreaker*

Punctuate It

Place dashes to indicate an interruption in speech or sudden change of thought in each sentence below.

1. "I can't go because " Jose moaned, stopping when his mother interrupted him.

2. Gerard said, "Once, when I was a kid, I "

3. "How do I I mean we get tickets to the game?" Ciara asked.

4. "Now class, today " the teacher stopped when the principal appeared.

Write It

Write 2 sentences using dashes to indicate an interruption in speech or sudden change of thought.

1. _____

_____

2. _____

_____

Hyphens Used with Numbers

Use hyphens to spell the numbers twenty-one through ninety-nine, to spell fractions, to place a number to a unit of measure, and to separate spans of numbers. A hyphen is about half the length of a dash. Do not place a space around hyphens. Use a dictionary to check the correct spelling of words.

Examples of Spelling Numbers Twenty-one through Ninety-nine: twenty-one, twenty-two, thirty-one, forty-four, fifty-five, sixty-four, seventy-seven

Examples of Spelled Out Fractions: one-half, one-third, three-fourths, one-fifth

Examples of Placing a Unit of Measure to a Number: 100-yard dash, 40-hour week, 70-foot trailer (Do not abbreviate words following the numbers.)

Examples of Spans of Numbers: 5-6 cats, 2001-2013, 3:15-4:15 p.m., pages 30-40

Finch's Landing consisted or three hundred and **sixty-six** steps down a high bluff and ending in a jetty.

Harper Lee, *To Kill a Mockingbird*

"A magnificent theft!" the policeman replied with gusto. "**Fifty-five** thousand pounds!"

Jules Verne, *Around the World in Eighty Days*

Mrs. Riggs asked us to read pages **21-25** in our history book.

Punctuate It

Place a hyphen correctly in the number words below.

1. fifty two miles

2. one half cup

3. pages 15 26

4. two fifths of a pie

5. 50 yard dash

6. 4:00 6:00 p.m.

7. forty one cats

8. 40 hour week

9. 2016 2017

Write It

Write 2 sentences using hyphens when spelling out fractions, the numbers twenty-one through ninety-nine, when placing a number to a unit of measure, or when writing spans of numbers.

1. _____

_____

2. _____

_____

Hyphens Separate Some Compound Words

Use hyphens to separate some compound words. A hyphen is about half the length of a dash. Hyphens are often used in compound nouns, compound adjectives, ages used as adjectives before a noun, compounds with three or more words, and "improvised words." Do not place a space around hyphens. Use a dictionary to check the correct spelling of compound words.

Examples of Compound Nouns: great-grandmother, great-aunt, great-uncle, kid-gloves, mother-in-law, sister-in-law, brother-in-law

Examples of Compound Adjectives: big-ticket item, nine-foot fence, gold-filled bracelet, heavy-duty tires, low-budget movie, well-known actor

Examples of Age Adjectives used Before Nouns: one-year-old boy, eighty-five-year-old aunt, five-year-old daughter

Examples of Three Word Compound and Improvised Words: brother-in-law, mother-in-law, know-it-all, well-to-do, word-of-mouth

Today, however, though they were civil enough, the **field-mice** and **harvest-mice** seemed preoccupied.

Kenneth Grahame, *The Wind in the Willows*

Despite the gleeful shouting and **merry-go-round** music, he could not forget the soccer field at the end of the park: silent, waiting.

Jerry Spinelli, *Wringer*

At least she was cool in the air-conditioned bedroom she shared with their **seven-year-old** sister, Lizzie, and their grandma.

Suzanne Collins, *Gregor the Overlander*

Punctuate It

Place hyphens to connect the compound words below.

1. dark eyed girl   **3.** five year old boy   **5.** low budget movie

2. nine foot fence   **4.** brother in law   **6.** sixty six year old man

Write It

Write 2 sentences using hyphens to separate a compound noun, compound adjective, an age adjective before a noun, or a three word compound.

1. _____

_____

2. _____

_____

Hyphens Separate Some Prefixes and Root Words

Use hyphens between some prefixes and root words. A hyphen is about half the length of a dash. Use a dictionary to check the correct spelling of compound words.

Use a hyphen between prefixes joined to proper nouns or proper adjectives. **Examples:** un-American, pro-Canadian, trans-Atlantic, mid-July

Use a hyphen between the prefixes *self, great, half, all, and ex* when joined to a noun or adjective. **Examples:** all-inclusive, ex-marine, great-grandmother, half-brother, self-addressed

Use a hyphen to eliminate confusion when the prefix ends with the same vowel letter that the root word begins with. **Examples:** anti-inflammatory, co-opt, semi-invalid

"That's my father," Arrietty realized with a start, "my father talking to **Great-Aunt** Sophy or rather **Great-Aunt** Sophy talking to my father."

Mary Norton, *The Borrowers*

She stepped back and surveyed the **half-demolished** counter the way someone stands back to study a newly hung photograph.

Jennifer Cervantes, *Tortilla Sun*

We planned a Mexican vacation to an **all-inclusive** resort in **mid-July**.

Punctuate It
Place a hyphen between the prefix and root word in each example below.

1. ex president   **3.** mid Atlantic   **5.** great grandmother

2. semi invalid   **4.** self aware   **6.** half brother

Write It
Write 2 sentences using hyphens to separate a prefix from a root word.

1. _____

_____

2. _____

_____

Hyphens Separate Syllables, Words Spelled Out, and Letters Joined to Words

> Use hyphens to separate a word divided into syllables, words or letters that are spelled out, and a single capital letter joined to a word.
>
> **Examples of Syllables:** be-yond, awe-some, fan-tas-tic, won-der-ful
>
> **Examples of Letters or Words Spelled Out:** l-o-v-e, y-e-s, n-o, a-l-w-a-y-s
>
> **Examples of a Single Letter Joined to a Word:** T-shirt, U-turn, A-frame, V-neck

"**Won-a-pa-lei**," I answered, which as I have said, means The Girl with the Long Black Hair.

Scott O'Dell, *Island of the Blue Dolphin*

"Why not?" I asked, twisting a loose thread on the hem of my **T-shirt** around my pinky.

Jennifer Cervantes, *Tortilla Sun*

"**A-B-C**," said Boots, which is what she always said when she saw letters.

Suzanne Collins, *Gregor the Overlander*

Punctuate It
Place hyphens correctly in each sentence below.

1. Uncle Will built the A frame cabin.

2. My name is Coretta; it is spelled C o r e t t a.

3. Liliana greeted me with a friendly a lo ha.

4. Jamal wore his favorite V neck T shirt to school.

Write It
Write 2 sentences using hyphens to separate a word divided into syllables, letters or words that are spelled out, or a single capital letter joined to a word.

1. _____

_____

2. _____

_____

Hyphens Divide Words at the End of Lines

Use hyphens to divide words at the end of sentences when there is not enough space to write the complete word. Divide the word between syllables. Place a hyphen after the syllable. Place the remainder of the word on the next line. Do not divide a word leaving a single letter on a line.

Examples:

Incorrect: Lynn and Bryan decided to take a vacation to the Bahamas in A-
             pril or May. *Do not leave one letter alone on a line.*

Correct: Lynn and Bryan decided to take a vacation to the Bahamas in
             April or May.

Incorrect: On Wednesday afternoon, my mother and I shopped at the supe-
             rmarket. *Incorrectly divided between syllables.*

Correct: On Wednesday afternoon, my mother and I shopped at the super-
             market.

Punctuate It

Place hyphens correctly at the end of each line below.

1. Kim and Raul filled their shopping basket with fresh peaches, sweet straw
   berries, juicy pineapples, and yellow bananas.
2. When they arrived home, Kim sliced the juicy fruit and made a color
   ful fruit salad.
3. The sweet, fresh fruit salad was the perfect treat for a hot summer after
   noon.
4. Courtney planned the following weekend activities: exercising, shop
   ping, and swimming.

Write It

Write 2 sentences using hyphens to divide words at the end of each sentence when there is not enough space to write the complete word.

1. _____

   _____

2. _____

   _____

Apostrophes Show Possession

Use apostrophes with singular and plural nouns to indicate possession or ownership.

Singular Nouns: Place the apostrophe at the end of singular noun followed by the letter "s." This includes nouns ending in *s, x, z, ch, or sh*.

    dog's collar   car's tires   boss's desk   fox's den

Example: Mrs. Judd's class won the school spirit contest.

Plural Nouns: Place the apostrophe after the letter "s" in plural nouns.

    teachers' classrooms   flowers' petals   teams' uniforms

Example: The lions' cages were larger than the monkeys' cages.

The house which Tom's father lived in was up a foul little pocket called Offal Court, out of Pudding Lane.

Mark Twain, The Prince and the Pauper

During the first few days after the orphans' arrival at Count Olaf's, Violet, Klaus, and Sunny attempted to make themselves feel at home, but it was really no use.

Lemony Snicket, A Series of Unfortunate Events: The Bad Beginning

"Kids' names," said Merridew. "Why should I be Jack? I'm Merridew."

William Golding, Lord of the Flies

Punctuate It

Place an apostrophe correctly in the words below to show singular or plural possession.

1. Masons bike   3. two boys jackets   5. the cats paw

2. Moms car   4. the cooks recipe   6. five players hats

Write It

Write 2 sentences using contractions with apostrophes in the words.

1. _____

_____

2. _____

_____

Apostrophes Used in Contractions

Use apostrophes in contractions. Contractions are words formed by joining two words, and the newly formed word is shortened. An apostrophe is used to indicate that a letter or letters has been omitted in the newly formed word.

Examples of Common Contractions

Original Word	Contraction	Original Word	Contraction
are not	aren't	it is	it's
cannot	can't	it will	it'll
could have	could've	she will	she'll
could not	couldn't	she would	she'd
did not	didn't	they have	they've
he will	he'll	they will	they'll
he would	he'd	we will	we'll
I do	I 'd	we have	we've
I have	I 've	will not	won't
I will	I 'll	you have	you've

Punctuate It

Use the chart above to write the correct contraction for the words below.

1. I do_____   **3.** you have_____   **5.** she will_____

2. he will_____   **4.** will not_____   **6.** could not_____

Write It

Write 2 sentences using contractions with apostrophes in the words.

1. _____

_____

2. _____

_____

80

Apostrophes Used with Informal Contractions

Use apostrophes with some informal contractions. Informal contractions include vocabulary used casually by specific groups of people and those who live in specific geographical regions. These words are often formed by joining two words, and the newly formed word is shortened. An apostrophe is used to indicate that a letter or letters has been omitted in the newly formed word.

Examples of Informal Contractions

Contraction	Meaning	Contraction	Meaning
ain't	am not	jus'	just
bein'	being	mistakin'	mistaken
c'mon	come on	nothin'	nothing
comin'	coming	showin'	showing
doin'	doing	somethin'	something
diggin'	digging	stan'	stand
ever'body's	everybody	startin'	starting
'em	them	sure 'nuff	sure enough
fixin'	fixing	supposin'	supposing
gettin'	getting	tryin'	trying
goin'	going	we'all	we all
helpin'	helping	wishin'	wishing
I'ma	I am	y'all or ya'll	you all

"I guess you can come an' get me any time," he mumbled. "Anyway, I'm goin' to sleep."

Jack London, *White Fang*

"I ain't gonna say nothin'. Jus' gonna stan' there."

John Steinbeck, *Of Mice and Men*

"I wishin' ours was jus' startin'," sighed Jeremy.

Mildred B. Taylor, *Roll of Thunder, Hear My Cry*

Punctuate It
Use the chart above and write each word below as an informal contraction.

1. am not_____ **3.** going_____ **5.** I am_____

2. you all_____ **4.** being_____ **6.** nothing_____

Write It
Write 2 sentences using informal contractions with an apostrophe.

1. _____

_____

2. _____

_____

Pro Tip: Vary Sentence Type, Length, and Punctuation

Good writers use different sentence types, lengths, and punctuation to make their sentences and paragraphs more interesting. Notice how the professional writers below use long and short sentences with different types of punctuation to create drama, action, suspense, and humor. Notice how the punctuation affects the speed, tone, and mood of the sentence.

The butterfly. Of course! She had never bestowed the butterfly on him before, because it was new to him—and to her, too, with its damp, unfolding golden wings.

Lois Lowry, *Gosamer*

He passed another hole, and another, and another; and then—yes!—no!—yes! certainly a little narrow face, with hard eyes, had flashed up for an instant from a hole, and was gone.

Kenneth Grahame, *The Wind in the Willows*

He opened the door—and there they were! Beans. Mutto. Henry. Three grinning faces. Shoving wrapped gifts into his chest. Storming past him into his house, Beans bellowing, "Where's the grub?"

Jerry Spinelli, *Wringer*

"Lonely? Ha! Lonely? Not by a long shot. I've got my dog, and when I want to see people I just walk down to the harbor. When I want real quiet, I go on over to Wood Island."

Sharon Creech, *The Wanderer*

"Welcome!" he said. "Welcome to a new year at Hogwarts! Before we begin our banquet, I would like to say a few words. And here they are: Nitwit! Blubber! Oddment! Tweak! Thank you!"

J. K. Rowling, *Harry Potter and The Sorcerer's Stone*

Go home? How could he go home without his pockets full of gold nuggets? "Then I'm going on to California," the boy said. "I'm not turning back. No, sir." He wiped his nose. "But if you don't want me for a partner any more, why I'll—"

Sid Fleischman, *By the Great Horn Spoon!*

Pro Tip: Vary Sentence Type, Length, and Punctuation

Punctuate It

Now it's time to use everything you have learned. Place the correct punctuation in each sentence below. Place periods, exclamation points, question marks, dashes, commas, colons, ellipsis, or quotation marks as needed. Each paragraph requires several punctuation marks.

1. Look Jason yelled pointing at a bright light streaking across the dark evening sky What is it Where did it come from Where is it going Jason stared at the glowing flickering ball wondering if it could be one of the following a comet a meteor an asteroid or a rocket

2. Greg couldn't believe it Everyone was standing clapping and cheering as he crossed the finish line Had he won Yes He had won He had won his first marathon ever

3. Hey where did everyone go Katie called out looking around the room Chad Owen Rylan I was hoping that someone would help me with the cooking cleaning and vacuuming Unbelievable Everyone has left and I am here alone Well maybe I'll just relax today

4. Chores said Nick We have no time for chores It's Saturday and Erin and I have to take Kyla to soccer practice in the morning piano lessons at noon and a birthday party in the afternoon How can we finish chores Well we we can't There's no time No time for chores

5. Afraid Don't be Just do it Face your fears now right now and experience the danger the excitement and the adventure

Write It

Write a paragraph varying sentence type, length, and punctuation. Be creative and use what you have learned to *PUNCTUATE Like a Pro!*

_____

_____

_____

_____

_____

_____

Answer Key

Page 6

1. The Pacific Ocean is the largest ocean on Earth.

2. The two longest rivers in the world are the Nile and the Amazon.

3. Mount Everest is the tallest mountain in the world.

4. George Washington was the first president of the United States.

Page 7

1. Stop the bus at the next corner.

2. Eat all of your meat and vegetables.

3. Turn out the lights and close the door when you leave.

4. Please go straight home after school.

Page 8

1. Mister __Mr.__   **3.** Doctor __Dr.__   **5.** Saint __St.__

2. Senior __Sr.__   **4.** Avenue __Ave.__   **6.** October __Oct.__

Page 9

1. One by one the students fell asleep. First Jeff. Then Sal and Kira.

2. Trina ate the noodles but left the green things. Peas. Broccoli. Yuk!

3. The lights began to flicker. On. Off. On. Off.

4. Breathe in. Breathe out. Deep breath. Good job!

Page 10

1. The barking dog chased Ben all the way home!

2. Thomas misplaced his wallet and his car keys!

3. Nick and Erin won a million dollars in the lottery last night!

4. Sue couldn't believe she had won the spelling bee!

Page 11

1. Pack your bags and get out this minute!

2. Catch the baseball!

3. Watch out for that car!

4. Hurry up and get ready for school!

Page 12

1. Awesome! Our science project won first place.

2. Bravo! Bravo! That was a wonderful speech.

3. Oh no! I tripped and dropped my computer.

4. Yes! Yes! We won the dance competition.

Page 13

1. Go get help! Go! Go! Go!

2. Never! Never! Never in a hundred years!

3. We discovered gold! Gold! Precious gold!

4. We're rich! We're rich! Rich! Rich! Rich!

Page 14

1. What time does the basketball game start tonight?

2. Can Ricardo pick up bananas at the grocery store?

3. Do you know how to bake chocolate chip cookies?

4. Why? Why can't I go to the football game?

Answer Key

Page 16

1. Wow! That was the best movie I have ever seen.
2. Do you know what time the bus arrives?
3. Watch out! The huge bear is running our way!
4. Alec and Megan will go snow skiing today.
5. Will Jane and Chuck attend the volleyball clinic?
6. Yahoo! Janelle made it to the top of the hill.
7. Mrs. Martell asked everyone to turn in their homework.
8. Where should we go for lunch?
9. Please! Please! Please let me go to the game!
10. Carol and Michael attended the jazz concert.
11. What time should we leave for our appointment?
12. Nick and Erin walked Ollie for one mile.
13. Ouch! I twisted my ankle.
14. No! No! No! I won't do it!

Page 17

1. Abraham Lincoln was born on February 12, 1809, in Kentucky.
2. Lincoln was elected president on November 6, 1860.
3. On January 1, 1863, President Lincoln issued the Emancipation Proclamation.
4. The Declaration of Independence was signed on July 4, 1776.

Page 18

1. The White House is located in Washington, D.C.
2. President Obama was born in Honolulu, Hawaii, in 1961.
3. Disneyland Park is located in Anaheim, California.
4. Paris, France, is the most popular tourist city in the world.

Page 19

1. "Can you pick me up at noon, Lucy?" asked Gin.
2. "If you want, Jon, I can help you," offered Maria.
3. "Sam, will you mow the lawn today?"
4. "Are you home yet, Jana?" asked Annie.

Page 20

1. Julio Martinez, D.D.S., is the best dental surgeon in our town.
2. Rina Singh, R.N., received her nursing degree in 2014.
3. Susan Crow, Ph.D., gave an amazing lecture last week.
4. Our family doctor is Jamal James, M.D.

Page 21

1. Finally, Corey worked his way to the front of the lunch line.
2. Before long, Jamison reached the top of the huge hill.
3. After a long wait, Ming decided to walk home.
4. First, we have to mix the cake batter with the eggs.

Page 22

1. Exhausted, cold, and wet, the hiker shuffled through the deep snow.
2. Tired and muddy, Mateo wiped the sweat from his brow.
3. Tiny, fragile, and afraid, Mina froze as the shadowy figure approached.
4. Stronger now, Edison felt he could conquer the world.

Page 23

1. Cautiously, the hikers climbed up the steep mountain.
2. Quietly, Jonah read the last few chapters of the book.
3. Happily, Sheila helped her mother wash the dinner dishes.
4. Slowly and tiredly, David walked off the soccer field.

Answer Key

Page 24

1. The basketball team, in fact, was ranked number one.

1. Therefore, everyone came to watch the game.

2. Consequently, there weren't enough seats for all of the fans.

3. Additional seating, finally, was added in the gymnasium.

Page 25

1. Hey, let's go to the movies today.

2. Oh no, I can't go swimming because I have soccer practice.

3. Well, we can all go on vacation together in July.

4. Huh, what did you say?

Page 26

1. Facing his fears, Jerome climbed back on the wild bronco.

2. Realizing he was lost, Hiram sat down and waited for help.

3. Seated quietly at her desk, Nan tried to solve the math problem.

4. Running to the sink, Austin washed the mud off of his dirty hands.

Page 27

1. With perfect form, Saraya completed her swan dive.

2. In the final analysis, we agreed that her dive was the best.

3. At the end of the day, the judges awarded her first prize.

4. With a wide grin, she proudly displayed her trophy.

Page 28

1. After Owen completed his assignment, he went to lunch.

2. Because it was raining, Violet brought her umbrella to school.

3. While Sonya cleaned the table, her sister washed the dishes.

4. Since Rylan's team won the game, they celebrated at the pizza parlor.

Page 29

1. The warm, sweet sugar cookie tasted delicious.

2. Mindy hugged the sweet, tiny kitten.

3. Sophia shaped the soft, cool clay into round balls.

4. The loud, playful monkey swung from limb to limb.

Page 30 (Any –ly adverb for 1 and 2. Any adjective for 3 and 4).

1. <u>Carefully</u>, <u>cautiously</u>, the rescuers scaled the steep cliff.

2. <u>Happily</u>, <u>quietly</u>, Avery finished the gardening.

3. Tristan watched the <u>tall</u>, <u>mysterious</u> man enter the room.

4. The children drank the fruit juice, <u>cool</u> and <u>refreshing</u>.

Page 31

1. Serena, Sasha, and Tina play on the same softball team.

2. Mom bought vanilla, chocolate, and strawberry ice cream.

3. Benjamin Franklin was an author, printer, scientist, and politician.

4. Greg taught the puppy to sit, stay, and heel.

Page 32

1. Pablo grabbed his lunch, lined up, and walked to the cafeteria.

2. Tam raised her hand, answered the question, and patted herself on the back.

3. Stefan jumped on his bike, rode down the street, and turned left at the corner.

4. Haley dug a hole, planted seeds, and covered the seeds with soil.

Answer Key

Page 33

1. Manny played baseball on Monday, and he practiced football on Tuesday, but he rested on Wednesday.

2. The barking dog chased the cat across the yard, but the feline scurried up a tree, so the canine gave up and trotted home.

3. Hungry lions roared in their cages, and playful monkeys chattered on tree limbs, but the tall giraffes grazed quietly.

4. Vanessa wanted to go to the movies, but she had homework to finish, so she stayed home.

Page 34

1. Wynton Marsalis, in my opinion, is the best trumpet player of all time.

2. He is a talented musician, in fact, who teaches and composes music.

3. Marsalis, I believe, was inspired by some of the great horn players of the past.

4. He is known, of course, throughout the music world.

Page 35

1. John Adams, our second president, was a leader of the American Revolution.

2. We went to Yosemite, a national park in California, for our vacation.

3. Kai wanted to buy a new motorcycle, one with a fast engine.

4. Mr. Sanchez, our geometry teacher, taught algebra last year.

Page 36

1. Kira, who was thirteen, liked her job delivering newspapers.

2. Milo climbed the tree, slowly and carefully, to rescue the cat.

3. The old clock, a gift from my mother, had stopped working.

4. Sarina ate her dessert, a hot fudge sundae, after eating dinner.

Page 37

1. Everyone wanted to go to the movies, even Justin.

2. Liza wanted to be dropped off at 1 p.m., not 2 p.m.

3. Carlos didn't want to go home, not now or ever.

4. Josh hoped to attend the science camp this year, not next year.

Page 38

1. Melanie drives a sports car, but her sister drives an old truck.

2. Geno is a baseball pitcher, and his brother is a catcher.

3. School was scheduled for half-day, so students left at noon.

4. Phil enjoys traveling by car, but Mary prefers traveling by plane.

Page 39

1. When Malik finished his lunch, he went outside and played tag.

2. Since everyone had gone home, Melania left work early.

3. Because it was raining, Tisha wore her new raincoat to school.

4. After Kinsley finished her clarinet lesson, she packed up her instrument and walked home.

Page 40

1. Lily, whose father was a dentist, planned on attending medical school.

2. The van, which held six passengers, was painted bright red.

3. The executive, who was very kind, let employees leave early.

4. The painting, which was sold at the auction, had two colors.

Page 42

1. When Jay finished his homework, he went outside; he rode his bike around the neighborhood.

2. Since everyone had gone home, Melia left work early, so she could beat the rush hour traffic.

3. Because it was raining, Tanya wore her new rain boots; her feet stayed warm and dry all day.

4. After Libby finished her guitar lesson, she went to Briana's house, and they finished their school project.

Answer Key

Page 43

1. Marcus ate his lunch; he went outside when he was finished.
2. Everyone had gone home; therefore, Mel left work early because she wanted to beat the rush hour traffic.
3. Trevor attends a military academy; he hopes to become an officer when he graduates.
4. Carson played piano; meanwhile, his brother played the drums while listening to rock music.

Page 44

1. Brian finished his lunch, so he went outside since it was a warm day.
2. Everyone had gone home; therefore, Mel left work early because she wanted to beat the rush hour traffic.
3. Tisha wore her new rain boots; her feet stayed warm and dry when she walked home in the rain.
4. Marla finished her clarinet lesson, so she went to Briana's house since they had a project to finish.

Page 45

1. Jacob ate his lunch, which he gobbled down, so he could go outside.
2. The fox slowly approached, which I didn't like, so I quietly backed away.
3. Misha wore her new rain boots, which were bright yellow, and her feet stayed warm and dry.
4. Kyla liked Sam, who was her best friend; they walked to school together every day.

Page 46

1. The famous movie star signed autographs, and she smiled for the camera as the photographer took several pictures.
2. When the Corvette sped around the corner, the driver hit the brakes, and the sports car came to a sudden stop.
3. Because it snowed all day, Susan stayed home, so she decided to watch a movie.
4. Rebecca wanted to ride her new bike; however, her mother said she would have to wait because it was too cold.
5. Since their team won, the players celebrated; they went out for pizza.
6. When Maria returned home, she headed straight to the kitchen because she was hungry.
7. The teacher held up an old object, which looked like a plate, and she asked the class to examine it.
8. Mira traveled by boat around the world, which was her life-long dream; it took fifty days.
9. When she reached the Panama Canal, it was amazing to see how the boats were lifted up and down the canal; in fact, even huge cargo ships could pass through.

Page 47

1. "Jamie is ready to go home now," Mia announced.
2. Ed asked, "May I have a ride to school?"
3. "Most volunteers," stated Jamal, "like to work in the morning."
4. "We will leave for the play at noon," announced Martina.

Page 48

1. "I have to study," complained Chen, opening his math book.
2. "Let's hurry," said Keenan, looking down at his watch, "so we can catch the next bus."
3. "Everyone is going to the dance tonight," Hazel explained, hoping her mother would let her go.
4. "I hope I win the spelling bee," said Omar, crossing his fingers for good luck.

Page 49

1. The train left late; it arrived early.
2. Cora played violin; her sister played piano; her brother played drums.
3. School begins in August; it ends in June.
4. Manuela baked chocolate cupcakes; her mother iced them.

Answer Key

Page 50

1. The kitten chased the mouse; however, the mouse escaped.

2. Alyssa loved to play tennis; therefore, she played every day.

3. Shira didn't eat breakfast; as a result, she had no energy.

4. Marty was a quick starter; however, he was a slow finisher.

Page 51

Edwin's walls were decorated with famous athletes like: baseball players Babe Ruth, Jackie Robinson, and Hank Aaron; football players Joe Montana, Bart Star, and Tony Romo; and basketball players Michael Jordan, Stephen Curry, Kevin Durant, and LeBron James.

Page 52

1. Kendra bought everything needed to make the cake: flour, sugar, vanilla, eggs, butter, and salt.

2. Bradley made a list of the cities he would visit as follows: Paris, London, New York, Tokyo, and Moscow.

3. The colorful bouquet of flowers included: red roses, yellow daffodils, pink carnations, and white lilies.

4. Kim and Ken considered the following names for their baby: Kayden, Kenzley, Katelynn, or Kendra.

Page 53

1. Tami crossed the finish line in record time: one minute even.

2. No one heard it or saw it coming: a swift moving avalanche.

3. Henry didn't want anyone to know his secret: he had lied.

4. Marsha couldn't believe what she had found: a fifty-dollar bill.

Page 54

1. Many soldiers carry the words of Mark Twain with them into battle: "Courage is resistance to fear, mastery of fear, not absence of fear."

2. Albert Einstein, the famous physicist, once stated: "If you are out to describe the truth, leave elegance to the tailor."

3. Sir Isaac Newton's third law of motion states: "For every action, there is an equal and opposite reaction."

4. Our first president, George Washington, once said: "The Constitution is the guide which I never will abandon."

Page 55 (Colons after Greetings in Business Letters)

1. Dear Mrs. Jones: **3.** To Whom It May Concern: **5.** Dear Sir:

2. Dear Rev. Roberts: **4.** Dear Dr. Singh: **6.** Dear Ms. Li:

Page 55 (Colons in Clock Time)

1. 9:30 a.m. **2.** 12:30 p.m. **3.** 8:00 a.m. **4.** 10:00 p.m.

Page 56

1. "Have a nice day," Manny shouted, "see you tomorrow."

2. Elise asked, "Does anyone want to play basketball at recess?"

3. The teacher announced, "Everyone passed the math test!"

4. "What time does the soccer game start?" Lisa asked.

Page 57

1. "I heard Dad say, 'wash the car,'" Dion announced.

2. "Mario said, 'meet at ten sharp'!" Shannon yelled.

3. "Did Shirley say, 'it cost five dollars'?" asked Tim.

4. "Kyle said, 'put two cookies' in his lunch," Josie said.

Answer Key

Page 58

1. According to *Facts.com,* "Istanbul, Turkey, is the only city in the world with land on two continents."

2. *Life Magazine* recently reported that "Elizabeth Taylor had appeared on the cover more than any other celebrity."

3. A 2015 NASA study reported "an increase in Antarctic snow is adding enough ice to the continent to outweigh losses in thinning glaciers."

4. April's *Amazing Animals Magazine* reported that "the fastest land animal, the cheetah, was clocked at seventy miles per hour."

Page 59

1. Janelle thought it was a "bummer" that the party was cancelled.

2. Nina liked her costume and "glitzy" jewelry.

3. Taj bought a "cool" looking red sports car.

4. Aunt Barb likes to say "okie-dokie" when she means okay.

Page 60

1. Joni's favorite poem is "Phenomenal Woman" by Maya Angelou.

2. The short story "Rapunzel" is a well-known children's fairy tale.

3. The Beatles released the song "Hey Jude" in 1968.

4. "The Road Not Taken" is Robert Frost's most famous poem.

Page 61

1. The tiny puppy barked, "Arff, arff, arff."

2. When the mouse jumped on Sara's book, she screeched, "Ahhhhhh!"

3. The squirrel scurried up the tree squealing, "Eeek, eek, eek."

4. "Oink, oink, oink," the hungry pig snorted.

Page 62

1. Romeo and Juliet is my favorite Shakespeare play.

2. The children's book Charlotte's Webb is a wonderful story.

3. The movie Jurassic Park was filmed in Hawaii.

4. The Lion King is a popular children's movie.

Page 63

1. My grandfather traveled on the Queen Mary passenger ship.

2. Vincent van Gogh painted Starry Night in 1889.

3. The space shuttle Discovery completed thirty-nine flights.

4. Leonardo da Vinci began painting the Mona Lisa in 1503.

Page 65 (Any appropriate word will word).

1. Chip told Cathy he *wanted* to win the golf tournament.

2. Sophia found *twenty* dollars at the bottom of her purse!

3. "You did *what?*" Francis asked, staring at her friend.

4. Lorraine couldn't believe her eyes when she saw a *dragon!*

Page 66 (Any appropriate sound word will work)

1. Aliyah tiptoed across the *creaky* wooden floor.

2. Lorenzo jumped off the slide and landed with a *thud!*

3. *Roar!* A loud animal noise could be heard from the forest.

4. Liam stuck a pin in the balloon and it burst with a *POP!*

Answer Key

1. The sail fish (not the shark) is the fastest sea animal.
2. George Washington (1732-1799) was America's first president.
3. The White House (a huge mansion) took eight years to build.
4. The Space Shuttle Discovery (first launched in 1984) was the third space shuttle orbiter to fly in space.

Page 68
1. Brenda agreed to pick up supplies for (1) Kendra, (2) Maryanne, (3) Sybil, and (4) Tara.
2. Lily counted her change and found (a) two quarters, (b) three dimes, (c) five nickels, and (d) ten pennies.
3. The painter purchased the following supplies (a) one gallon of paint, (b) two rollers, (c) one paint tarp, and (d) three brushes.
4. I can think of three ways to be healthier (1) eat nutritious foods, (2) drink twenty ounces of water daily, and (3) exercise four days a week.

Page 70
1. "Why did this have to happen? Why did...?"
2. "It won't work. I can't hold..." Jessica screamed.
3. "I am not a thief. I am not..." cried Joel.
4. "Mom, I need school supplies, but..." Enzo hesitated.

Page 71 (Any response like the one below will work)
In *A Tale of Two Cities* written by Charles Dickens, he begins the novel with these famous words: "It was the best of times, it was the worst of times, it was the age of wisdom...."

Page 72
1. The prince had no idea—not a hint—that he had been tricked.
2. All children—naughty or nice—will receive a gift.
3. Jordan couldn't believe his luck—his bad luck.
4. It took time—a very long time—to reach the top of Mt. Everest.

Page 73
1. "I can't go because—" Jose moaned, stopping when his mother interrupted him.
2. Gerard said, "Once, when I was a kid, I—"
3. "How do I—I mean we—get tickets to the game?" Ciara asked.
4. "Now class, today—" the teacher stopped when the principal appeared.

Page 74
1. fifty-two miles	**4.** two-fifths of a pie	**7.** forty-one cats
2. one-half cup	**5.** 50-yard dash	**8.** 40-hour week
3. pages 15-26	**6.** 4:00-6:00 p.m.	**9.** 2016-2017

Page 75.
1. dark-eyed girl	**3.** five-year-old boy	**5.** low-budget movie
2. nine-foot fence	**4.** brother-in-law	**6.** sixty-six-year-old man

Page 76
1. ex-president	**3.** mid-Atlantic	**5.** great-grandmother
2. semi-invalid	**4.** self-aware	**6.** half-brother

Page 77
1. Uncle Will built the A-frame cabin.
2. My name is Coretta; it is spelled C-o-r-e-t-t-a.
3. Liliana greeted me with a friendly a-lo-ha.
4. Jamal wore his favorite V-neck T-shirt to school.

Answer Key

Page 78

1. Kim and Raul filled their shopping basket with fresh peaches, sweet strawberries, juicy pineapples, and yellow bananas.
2. When they arrived home, Kim sliced the juicy fruit and made a colorful fruit salad.
3. The sweet, fresh fruit salad was the perfect treat for a hot summer afternoon.
4. Courtney planned the following weekend activities: exercising, shopping, and swimming.

Page 79

1. Mason's bike	3. two boys' jackets	5. the cat's paw
2. Mom's car	4. the cook's recipe	6. five players' hats

Page 80

1. I do __I'd__	3. you have __you've__	5. she will __she'll__
2. he will __he'll__	4. will not __won't__	6. could not __couldn't__

Page 81

1. am not __ain't__	3. going __goin'__	5. I am __I'ma__
2. you all __ya'll__	4. being __bein'__	6. nothing __nothin'__

Page 83

1. "Look!" Jason yelled, pointing at a bright light streaking across the dark evening sky. "What is it? Where did it come from? Where is it going?" Jason stared at the glowing, flickering ball, wondering if it could be one of the following: a comet, a meteor, an asteroid, or a rocket.
2. Greg couldn't believe it. Everyone was standing, clapping, and cheering as he crossed the finish line. Had he won? Yes! He had won! He had won his first marathon ever.
3. "Hey, where did everyone go?" Katie called out, looking around the room. "Chad? Owen? Rylan? I was hoping that someone would help me with the cooking, cleaning, and vacuuming. Unbelievable! Everyone has left, and I am here alone. Well, maybe I'll just relax today."
4. "Chores!" said Nick. "We have no time for chores! It's Saturday, and Erin and I have to take Kyla to soccer practice in the morning, piano lessons at noon, and a birthday party in the afternoon. How can we finish chores? Well, we...we can't! There's no time. No time for chores."
5. Afraid? Don't be. Just do it! Face your fears now—right now—and experience the danger, the excitement, and the adventure.

Bibliography

Chicago Manual of Style Online. 16th edition. Chicago: University of Chicago Press, 2010. http://www.chicagomanualofstyle.org.

Hixon, Mamie. *The Essentials of English Language.* New Jersey: Research & Education Association, 2007.

Straus, Jane. *The Blue Book of Grammar and Punctuation.* San Francisco: Josey-Bass, 2014.

Recommended Reading and Works Cited

Alcott, Louisa May. *Little Women*. London: Hesperus Press, 2014.

Braun, Lilian Jackson. *The Cat Who Had 60 Whiskers*. New York: Penguin Group, 2007.

Carroll, Lewis. *Alice's Adventures in Wonderland*. Princeton: Princeton University Press, 2015.

Cervantes, Jennifer. *Tortilla Sun*. San Francisco: Chronicle Book, 2010.

Cleary, Beverly. *Jean and Johnny*. New York: HarperCollins Publishers, 1959.

Collier, James Lincoln., and Christopher Collier. *My Brother Sam is Dead*. New York: Simon & Schuster, 1974.

Collins, Suzanne. *Gregor the Overlander*. New York: Scholastic Press, 2003.

Creech, Sharon. *The Wanderer*. New York: Harper Collins Publishers, 2000.

Curtis, Christopher Paul. *Bud, Not Buddy*. New York: Delacorte Press, 1999.

Dahl, Roald. *James and the Giant Peach*. New York: Penguin Group, 1961.

Farley, Walter. *The Black Stallion*. New York: Random House, 1941.

Fleischman, Sid. *By the Great Horn Spoon!* New York: Hachette Book Group, 1963.

Forbes, Esther. *Johnny Tremain*. New York: Houghton Mifflin Company, 1943.

Golding, William. *Lord of the Flies*. New York: Penguin Group, 1954.

Grahame, Kenneth. *The Wind in the Willows*. New York: Random House, 1993.

Green, John. *Paper Towns*. New York: Dutton Books, 2008.

Green, John. *The Fault in Our Stars*. New York: Dutton Books, 2012.

Hawthorne, Nathaniel. *The Scarlet Letter*. New York: Oxford University Press, 1962.

Horowitz, Anthony. *Stormbreaker*. New York: Philomel, 2006.

Kafka, Franz. *Amerika*. New York: Schocken Books Inc., 1946.

Kipling, Rudyard. *The Jungle Book*. New York: Penguin Books, 1987.

Lee, Harper. *To Kill a Mockingbird*. New York: HarperCollins Publishers, 1960.

Lewis, C. S. *The Silver Chair*. New York: Harper Collins, 1953.

London, Jack. *The Call of the Wild*. New York: Penguin Group, 1991.

London, Jack. *White Fang*. New York: Penguin Group, 1991.

Lowry, Lois. *Gosamer*. New York: Random House, 2006.

Lowry, Lois. *The Giver*. New York: Houghton Mifflin Harcourt Publishing, 1993.

Montgomery, Lucy Maud. *Anne of Green Gables*. New York: Sterling Publishing Company, 2004.

Morpurgo, Michael. *War Horse*. New York: Scholastic Press, 1982.

Norton, Mary. *The Borrowers*. New York: Harcourt Books, 1953.

O'Dell, Scott. *Island of the Blue Dolphins*. Boston: Houghton Mifflin, 1960.

Olson, Tod. *Lost in the Pacific, 1942*. New York: Scholastic, 2016.

Paulsen, Gary. *Hatchet*. New York: Simon & Schuster, 1987.

Riordan, Rick. *The Heroes of Olympus: The Lost Hero*. New York: Hyperion, 2010.

Rowling, J. K. *Harry Potter and the Half-Blood Prince*. New York: Arthur A. Levine Books, 2005.

Rowling, J. K. *Harry Potter and the Sorcerer's Stone*. New York: Arthur A. Levine Books, 1999.

Saroyan, William. *The Human Comedy*. New York: Harcourt, 1971.

Sewell, Anna. *Black Beauty*. New York: Sterling Publishing Company, 2004.

Snicket, Lemony. *A Series of Unfortunate Events, The Bad Beginning*. New York: Harper Trophy, 1999.

Spark, Muriel. *The Prime of Miss Jean Brodie*. New York: Harper Perennial, 2009.

Spinelli, Jerry. *Wringer*. New York: Harper Collins, 1997.

Steinbeck, John. *Of Mice and Men*. New York: Viking Press, 1963.

Stevenson, Robert Louis. *Treasure Island*. New York: Penguin Book, 2009.

Taylor, Mildred D. *Roll of Thunder, Hear My Cry*. New York: Phyllis Fogelman Books, 2001.

Tolkien, J. R. R. *The Hobbit*. Boston: Houghton Mifflin, 2001.

Tolkien, J. R. R. *The Lord of the Rings*. Boston: Houghton Mifflin, 2005.

Twain, Mark. *The Prince and the Pauper*. New York: Random House, 1979.

Verne, Jules. *Around the World in Eighty Days*. New York: Bantam Books, 1984.

White, E. B. *Charlotte's Web*. New York: Harper Collins Publishers, 1999.

White, E. B. *The Trumpet of the Swan*. New York: Harper & Row, 1970.

White, T.H. *The Sword in the Stone*. New York: Philomel Books, 1993.

Wiesel, Elie. *Night*. New York: Hill and Wang, 2006.

Wilder, Laura Ingalls. *Little House on the Prairie*. New York: Harper Collins, 1981.

Yolen, Jane. *The Devil's Arithmetic*. New York: Penguin, 1988.

Made in the USA
San Bernardino, CA
24 August 2017